This book belongs to . . .

Aberdeenshire

3211363

D1139092

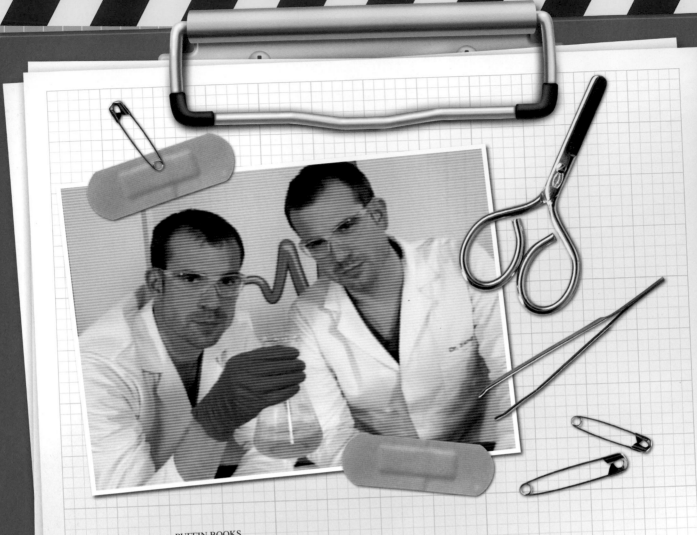

PUFFIN BOOKS

UK | USA | Canada | Ireland | Australia
India | New Zealand | South Africa

Puffin Books is part of the Penguin Random House group of companies
whose addresses can be found at global.penguinrandomhouse.com.

www.penguin.co.uk   www.puffin.co.uk   www.ladybird.co.uk

Penguin
Random House
UK

First published 2017
001

Written by Ben Elcomb, with consultation from
Dr Chris van Tulleken and Dr Xand van Tulleken
Designed and illustrated by Dan Green

Copyright for the individual photographs and medical illustrations remains
with the agents as indicated below
DK = DK Images, MT = Maverick Television

Printed in China

A CIP catalogue record for this book is available from the British Library

ISBN: 978–0–141–37597–7

All correspondence to:
Puffin Books
Penguin Random House Children's
80 Strand, London WC2R 0RL

Front cover MT, Back cover DK. Pages 2–7 DK/MT, 8 MT, 11–12 MT, 13 DK/MT, 14–20 MT, 21 DK/MT, 22–24 MT, 25 DK/MT, 26–28 MT, 29–30 DK/MT, 31 MT, 32 DK/MT, 33–34 MT, 36 MT, 37 DK, 38–39 MT, 40 DK/MT, 44–47 DK/MT, 50 DK, 51–53 DK/MT, 54–55 MT, 56 DK/MT, 57–58 MT, 60–66 DK/MT, 67 MT, 68 DK, 69–70 MT, 72 MT, 73 DK/MT, 76–77 DK/MT, 79–80 MT, 82–83 DK/MT, 84 DK, 85 MT, 86 DK/MT, 87 DK, 88 DK/MT, 90 DK/MT, 91–93 DK, 94 DK/MT, 95–96 MT, 98 MT, 99 DK, 101–108 MT, 109 DK, 110 DK/MT, 111–112 DK, 113 MT, 114–115 DK/MT, 116 DK, 118 DK, 119 DK/MT, 120 MT, 122 MT, 123–124 DK/MT, 125 MT, 126 DK/MT, 127–128 DK/MT, 129–130 DK/MT, 131 MT, 132 DK/MT, 134 DK/MT, 135 MT, 136 DK/MT, 138–139 DK/MT, 140 MT, 141–143 DK, 144 DK/MT, 145 MT, 146 DK, 147 DK/MT, 148–150 MT, 151–152 DK/MT, 154–155 MT, 156 DK/MT, 157–158 DK, 159–167 DK/MT, 169 DK, 170 DK/MT, 171 DK, 174–175 DK/MT

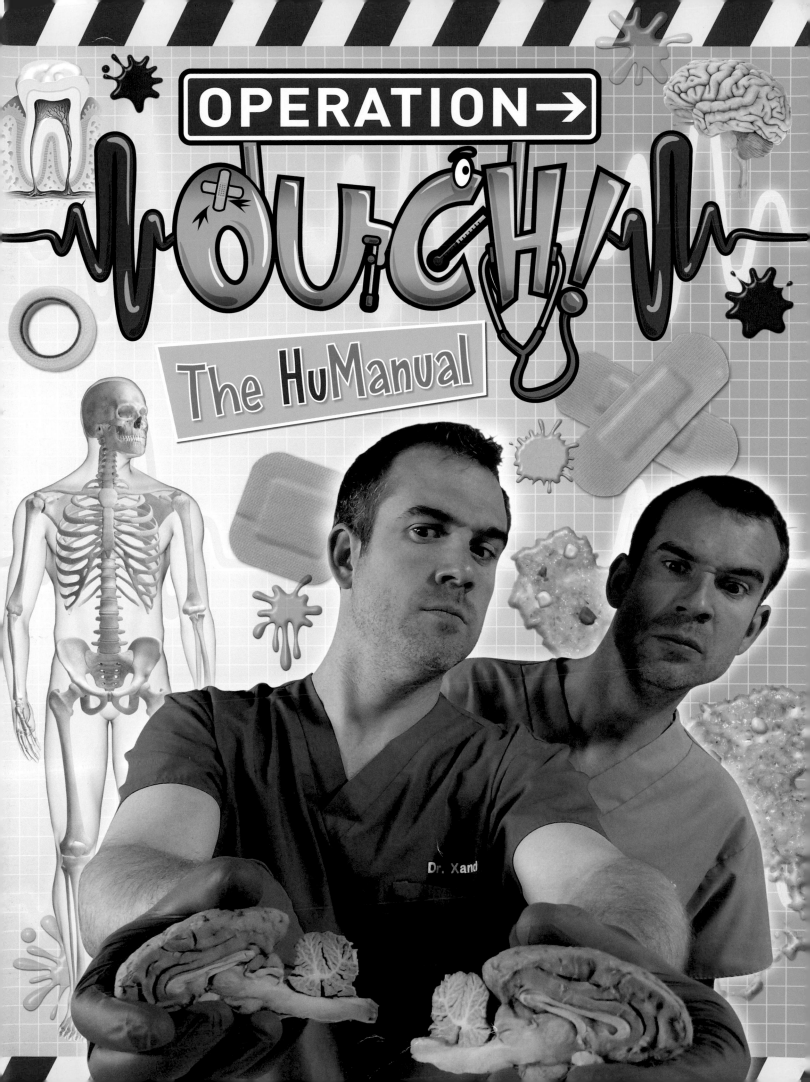

OPERATION →

OUCH!!!

The HuManual

Contents

Hello!

From cars to computers and televisions to tumble dryers, lots of things come with instructions to tell you how they work. But there's one amazing bit of kit we guarantee you already have that definitely didn't come with a manual.

Have you worked out what it is yet? That's right . . . it's your body!

Whether you read it cover to cover, or skip straight to the disgusting stuff about maggots on page 64, this manual will help you understand your body and make the best use of it that you can.

The two of us are still learning about human bodies and there is loads more for scientists to discover, but we hope you'll find this book to be a good start!

Chris   Xand

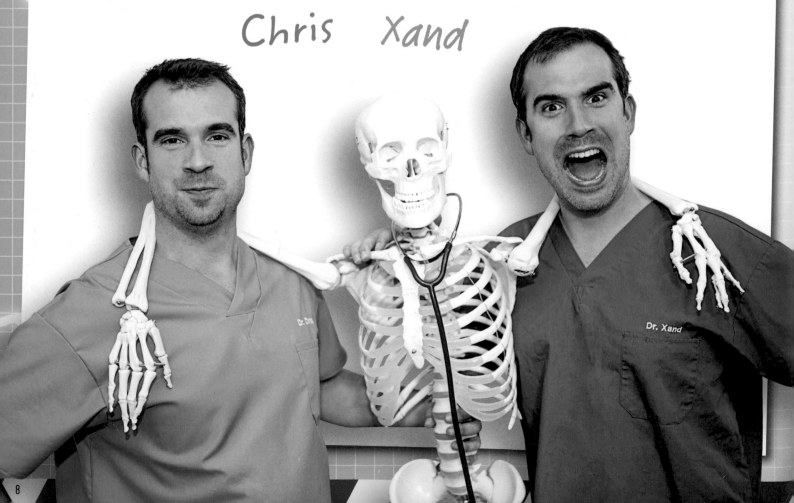

QUICK-START GUIDE

1. Wake up

2. Open eyes

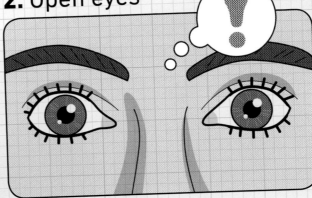

3. Live

4. Close eyes

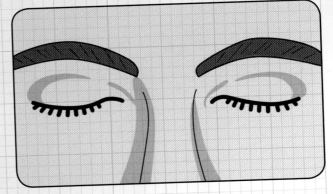

5. Sleep*

6. Repeat

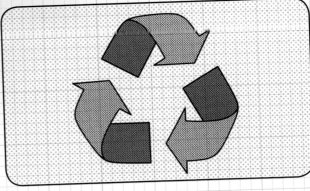

*Like lots of gadgets, the human body has a sleep function, but chances are, unless you've developed the amazing ability to sleep-read, you will be in awake mode right now.

AND THAT'S PRETTY MUCH ALL YOU NEED TO KNOW TO QUICK-START THE HUMAN MACHINE. EASY, RIGHT?

Disclaimer: This is a trivial examination of the human sleep cycle. Opening eyes is not a prerequisite for the visually impaired.

Human Prototypes

WHETHER IT'S MOBILE PHONES, CARS OR COMPUTERS, MANUFACTURERS ARE ALWAYS TRYING TO TWEAK AND IMPROVE THE THINGS WE USE IN OUR EVERYDAY LIVES. WELL, THE HUMAN BODY IS JUST THE SAME! IT'S BEEN THROUGH LOTS OF VERSIONS BEFORE WE ENDED UP LOOKING THE WAY WE DO TODAY. IT'S TIME TO MEET SOME OF THE FAMILY!

AUSTRALOPITHECUS AFARENSIS

- Lived between 4 and 2 million years ago
- Their brains were only slightly bigger than a chimp's
- Guzzled fruit, seeds, roots, insects and even small mammals
- Walked upright
- Average height: 1.10m

HOMO HABILIS

- Lived between 2.5 and 1.6 million years ago
- Had flatter faces and bigger brains than their ancestors
- These guys were the first hominids (the human line) to use tools
- Ate much more meat, meaning they consumed more nutrients (which helped their brains to get bigger)
- Average height: 1.30m

HOMO ERECTUS

- Lived between 1.8 million and 50,000 years ago
- The first ones to build shelters and, later, vessels to take to the sea
- Discovered fire and began to cook food. No more eating raw mammals – hooray!
- Hunted in groups, meaning they could catch bigger prey
- Average height: 1.60m

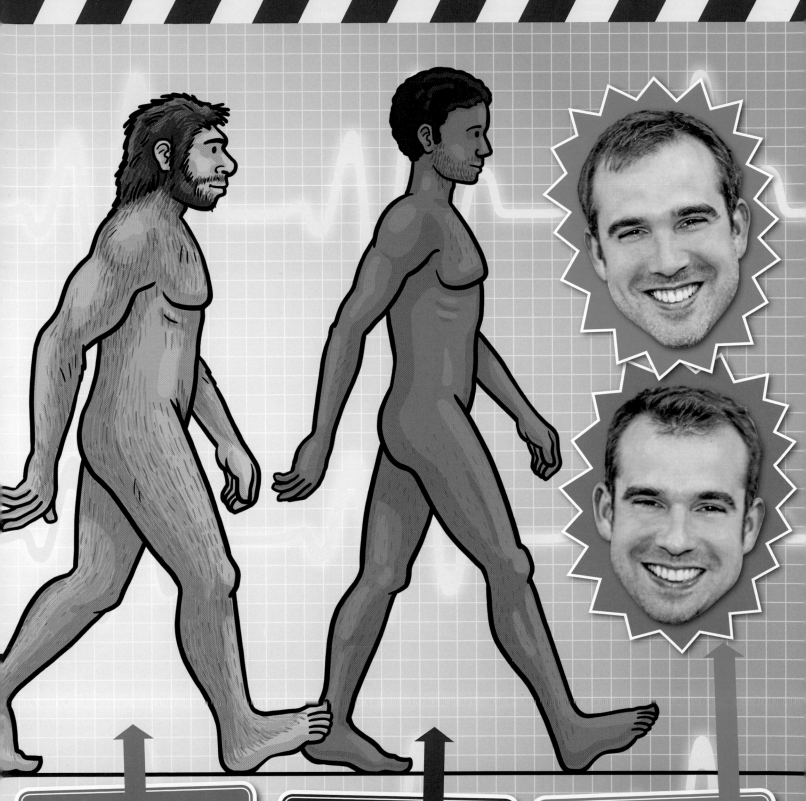

HOMO NEANDERTHALENSIS

- Lived between 230,000 and 28,000 years ago
- Short, stocky and strong, and able to survive in a colder climate
- Hunted larger prey using spears and stone axes
- Believed to be the first hominids to bury their dead
- Average height: 1.65m

HOMO SAPIENS – You!

- First appeared around 195,000 years ago
- Left Africa around 60,000 years ago
- Rapidly developed culture, tool use, hunting techniques and language
- Invented agriculture about 10,000 years ago, which led to the first cities
- Average height: 1.70m

DR CHRIS AND DR XAND

- First appeared around 30 to 40 years ago
- Presenters of CBBC's *Operation Ouch!*
- Most evolved homo sapiens ever. Possibly.
- Height: 1.85m

EYE EXAM →

XAND'S EYE

Iris

Pupil

Sclera

Lacrimal Caruncle

FACT
The muscles you use to blink are the fastest in your body.

DID YOU KNOW?
The colour of the iris depends on the amount of pigment in it. Xand has got a brown iris which means he's got lots of pigment. People with less pigment have lighter coloured eyes like blue or green.

Hole-y Moley!
The black pupil is actually a hole going right through to the back of the eyeball.

Lightbulb moment!
Your eyes use light to see. When you're somewhere dark like the cinema, your pupil becomes larger and opens up to let in as much light as possible, but if you go to a bright place like a sunny beach, your iris closes your pupil right down to let in less light because it doesn't need that much to see.

Your eye contains around 70% of your entire body's sensory receptors.

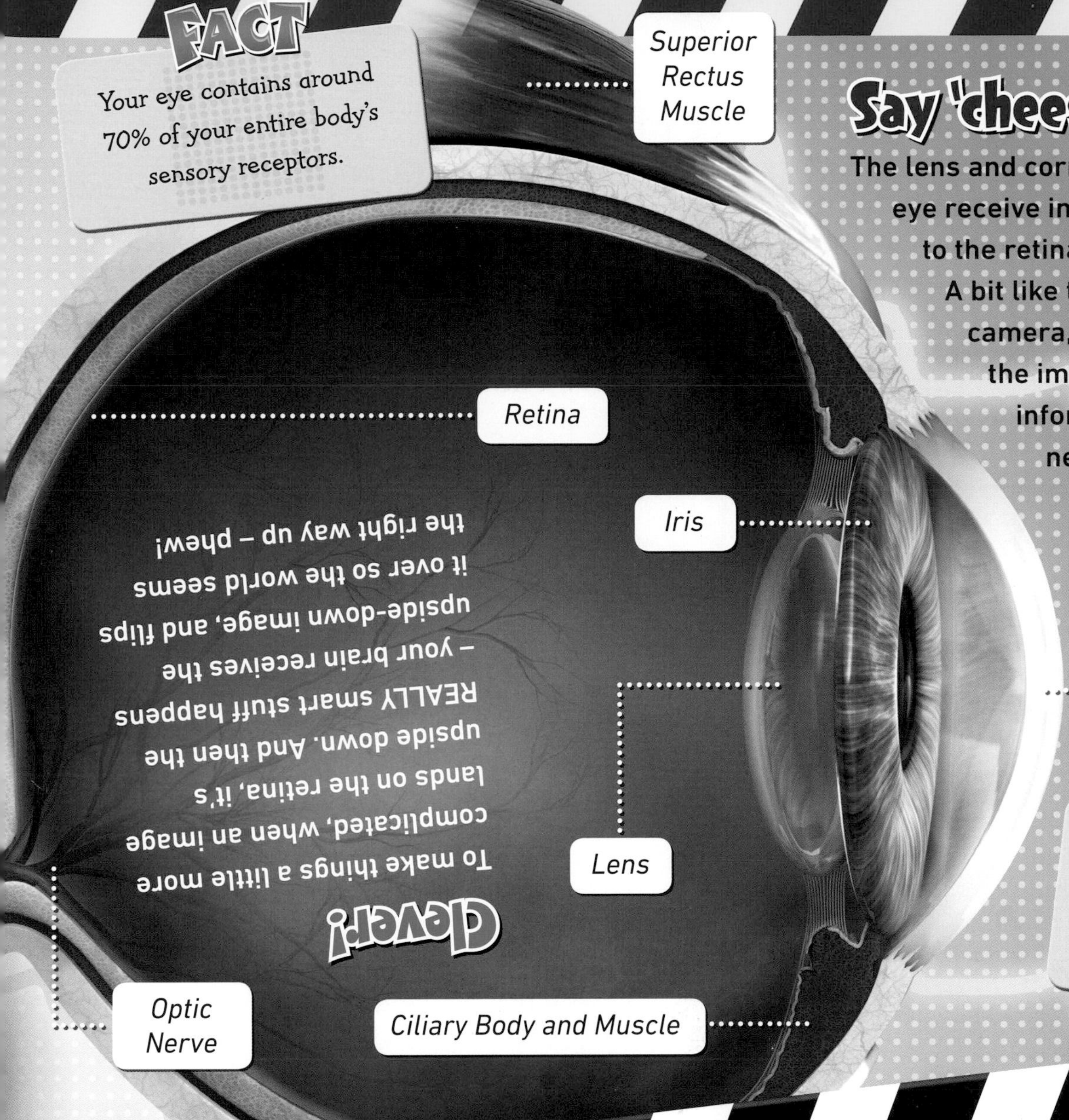

Superior Rectus Muscle

Say 'cheese'!

The lens and cornea at the front of your eye receive images and send them to the retina at the back of the eye. A bit like the sensor in a digital camera, the retina captures the image. It then sends the information along the optic nerve to a part of the brain called the occipital cortex for processing.

Retina

Iris

phew! – up way right the seems world the so over it flips and image, upside-down the receives brain your – happens stuff smart REALLY the then And down. upside it's retina, the on lands image an when complicated, more little a things make To

Clever!

Lens

Cornea

FACT

Your retina is incredibly sensitive to light. It can detect a single photon, the smallest amount of light possible!

Optic Nerve

Ciliary Body and Muscle

OUCH! Take #10:

We met a man called Antonio 'Popeye' Francis. Behind everyone's eyes lie six muscles controlling the movement of our eyeballs. Antonio has the amazing ability to contract these muscles, making his eyeballs appear to pop out. He can do it up to 200 times without needing a rest and he reckons they come out a whopping 12.3mm. Now that is amazing!

MINI Chris+Xand — BLACK EYED BOY

MINI CHRIS AND MINI XAND WERE PLAYING NICELY ON THEIR CONSOLE . . .

HOPE YOU'RE READY TO LOSE, MINI XAND . . .

AGAIN! HE SHOOTS, HE SCORES!

GOOOOOOOOAAAL!

OWWWWWWWW!

UH-OH . . . IT'S A TRIP TO A&E FOR MINI CHRIS AND MINI XAND.

SO, DO YOU BOYS WANT TO BE FOOTBALLERS WHEN YOU GROW UP?

NO, WE WANT TO BE DOCTORS!

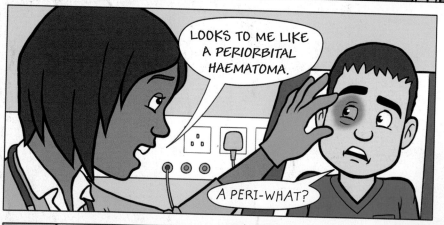

LOOKS TO ME LIKE A PERIORBITAL HAEMATOMA.

A PERI-WHAT?

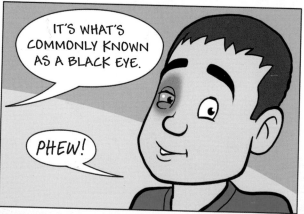

IT'S WHAT'S COMMONLY KNOWN AS A BLACK EYE.

PHEW!

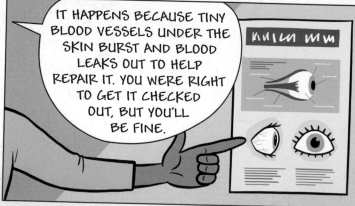

IT HAPPENS BECAUSE TINY BLOOD VESSELS UNDER THE SKIN BURST AND BLOOD LEAKS OUT TO HELP REPAIR IT. YOU WERE RIGHT TO GET IT CHECKED OUT, BUT YOU'LL BE FINE.

IMAGINE WORKING HERE! DO YOU THINK WE'LL EVER GET TO BE DOCTORS WHEN WE GROW UP?

'EYE' CERTAINLY HOPE SO!

DO TRY THIS AT HOME!

TAKE A LOOK AT THIS PHOTO. ALTHOUGH IT LOOKS A BIT STRANGE, YOU MAY RECOGNIZE THESE DOCTORS . . .

And rather good-looking they are too! Chris

Now stare at it for 30 seconds. Either count in your head, or get someone else to time it.

You are seeing this picture because your eyes are sending messages to your brain about the image. The longer you stare, the more tired your eyes become, so they eventually stop sending messages to your brain — but your brain remembers what the picture looks like.

WHEN 30 SECONDS ARE UP, LOOK AWAY AT A WALL OR A SHEET OF PLAIN PAPER AND YOU SHOULD STILL BE ABLE TO SEE CHRIS AND XAND!

FACT

Whilst reading this book, the muscles in your eyes are moving an astounding 170 times a minute!

WHAT DO YOU CALL A PIG WITH NO EYES?

I DON'T KNOW

A PG!

THESE EYE JOKES KEEP GETTING CORNEA . . .

The science bit!

This trick works because when you looked away, it took your brain a few moments to catch up and that's why you can still see Chris and Xand.

EYE Have a Problem

Don't be sad!

You don't just cry when you're upset. Your eyes use tears to flush out any debris that shouldn't be there. As your eye blinks, the liquid is spread around.

Wowza!

Your eye has the amazing ability to self-heal and send in fresh cells to mend a scratch, making your eye as good as new in about 24 hours!

Yuck!

Conjunctivitis symptoms include redness and a gunky yellow discharge! The 'itis' part means it's an inflammation, and it can have all sorts of causes ranging from an infection to radiation!

DID YOU KNOW?

Ever wondered why we have eyebrows and eyelashes? Well, they are the eyes' own line of defence, making sure that any invaders like dust or grit don't get into your eyes and cause any damage.

Creepy!

Right now, it's estimated that 10–20% of us could have tiny creatures living on our eyelashes – in fact some studies have put this number as high as 97%! Eyelash mites are tiny little critters who are only about a third of a millimetre long, and unless you have an allergic reaction to them, you may never know they are there. However, they aren't usually anything to worry about, and with that many of us potentially having them, you're in good company! Make mites your mates!

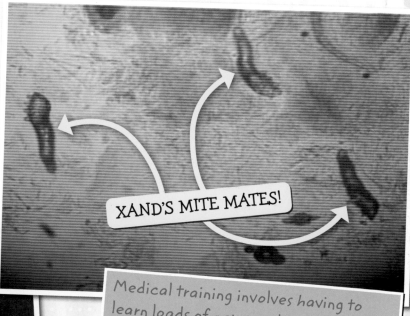

XAND'S MITE MATES!

Medical training involves having to learn loads of new words — around 2,000, which is like learning a whole other language! If you want to impress your mates, the scientific name for these little beasties is demodex mites!

Chris

Check This Out!

Xand met a girl called Grace who had what he described as *When-I-Fall-Asleep-And-Wake-Up-My-Eyes-Get-Really-Crusty-And-Red-itis.* This is more commonly known as blepharitis. But, as Grace found out, it's easy to treat – the first thing is to get a towel and just soak your eyelids, and that makes the crusty stuff a bit easier to remove.

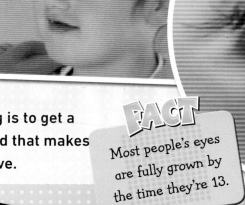

FACT

Most people's eyes are fully grown by the time they're 13.

Long-sighted people can see things that are a long distance away (like the horizon), but have trouble seeing things close to them. *Short-sighted* people can see things close to them (like a book), but have more difficulty with things in the distance.

Short-sightedness occurs when the eyeball grows too long from front to back. *Long-sightedness* happens when the eyeball is too short. Luckily, all it takes is a prescription pair of glasses or contact lenses to sort either problem out.

IMPORTANT SAFETY NOTICE! ⚠

AS WITH ANYTHING THAT'S WRONG WITH YOU, IF YOU'RE WORRIED OR UNSURE, IT'S BEST TO SPEAK TO AN ADULT AND GET IT CHECKED OUT BY A MEDICAL PROFESSIONAL.

FACT

Human eyes move over 100,000 times a day!

WHAT DID ONE EYE SAY TO THE OTHER?

I DON'T KNOW

BETWEEN YOU AND ME, SOMETHING SMELLS!

Eye Tech

FACT
Your eyes blink around twenty times a minute. That's over ten million times a year!

Cool!

Being twins, Chris' and Xand's eyes look similar, but they're not actually identical because eyes are as unique as fingerprints. That's why some airports use iris scanners to help identify people. Some mobile phone companies are also using similar tech to help you securely unlock your devices!

OUCH! Take #22:

Chris met blind Paralympian and multi-medal winner Tim Reddish. Tim was one of the first people in the world to receive a bionic eye! Sensors detect light coming into the eye and connect an electronic retina to the optic nerve, which in turn sends a signal to the brain. Clever stuff, huh?

OUCH! Take #73:

Chris met Ryan, one of the 25,000 blind and partially sighted children in the UK. Ryan showed Chris a really useful gadget called a liquid level indicator. Not the catchiest title, but it does what it says! With the liquid level indicator in a glass or cup, blind or partially sighted people like Ryan are able to pour a drink without spilling it everywhere because the clever gadget lets out a sound when the liquid is near the top.

BEEP! BEEP! BEEP!

FACT
An eyeball is about two thirds the size of a ping-pong ball!

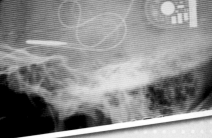

WHAT IS THE HARDEST-WORKING PART OF THE EYE?

I DON'T KNOW

THE PUPIL!

The Eye Test

CAN YOU SPOT THE EYEBALL AMONGST THE BEACH BALLS AT THE BEACH?

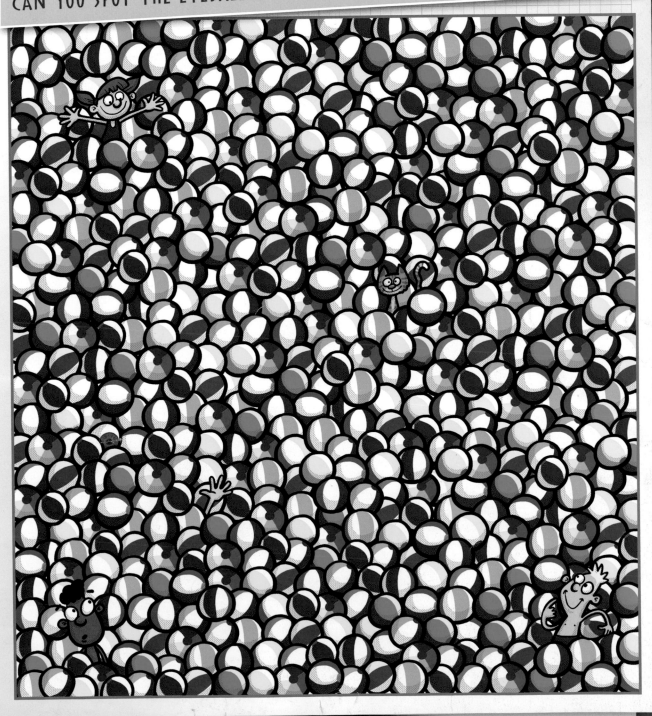

EAR YOU ARE →

This is Chris' ear. Or, at least, it's the first part. Although we refer to this wrinkly-looking flap of skin as an ear, it is only the first of three parts – the other bits are inside your head!

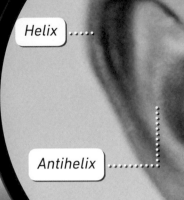

CHRIS' EAR

Helix

Tragus

Antihelix

Lobe

DID YOU KNOW?

The outer ear is a gristly skin-flap that helps to direct sound waves into the ear.

FACT
Your ears never stop growing!

FACT
The middle section of your ear (the tympanic membrane, behind the ear-drum) is only slightly larger than a pea!

FACT

Have your ears ever 'popped' on a plane? That's because of the effect of air pressure on your ear-drums. If your Eustachian tubes (which connect your middle ear to the back of your throat) don't properly regulate this pressure it can sometimes cause ear pain or discomfort. Some people find sucking on a boiled sweet, chewing on something or yawning helps. This will open the Eustachian tube and allow air to enter the middle ear. When outside pressure changes, the Eustachian tube supplies a bubble of air and the ears pop. When this happens, the air pressure goes back to normal.

POP! POP!

Hear Me Now!

Sounds are created when something makes a noise and sends vibrations and pressure waves through the air. The ear picks up these sounds, a bit like a satellite receiver, and sends them to the brain for analysis. The brain then compares this to other sounds it has heard before to identify what we are hearing.

FACT

A headmaster had a hair sprouting from his ear that was over 18cm long!

20

Going Deeper

The second part is the middle ear. This contains the ear-drum and three small bones called the ossicles. Sound is carried to the ear-drum, where the ossicles convert vibrations into movements . . .

Deep Inside

. . . and now we're at the inner ear, containing the cochlea and the semi-circular canals. The movements made by the ossicles send pressure waves through the fluid in the cochlea, which in turn sends signals to the brain.

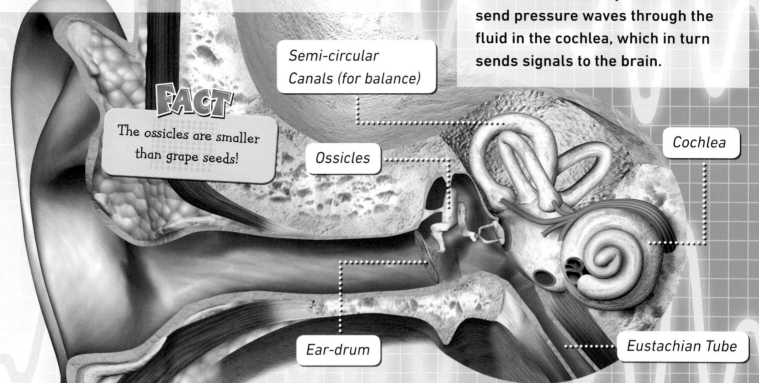

Semi-circular Canals (for balance)

FACT

The ossicles are smaller than grape seeds!

Ossicles

Cochlea

Ear-drum

Eustachian Tube

FACT

Your ears never stop hearing sounds. Your brain just ignores most noises when you sleep.

That would explain why Xand doesn't always wake up when his alarm goes off! Chris

The Beat of the Drum

The ear-drum really is like a very tiny drum! The ear-drum is a thin membrane that covers the end of the ear canal. When sound waves reach this membrane, it vibrates just like a real drum.

Tiny Tools

The parts of the ossicles are named after things you wouldn't usually expect to find in your body – the hammer, the anvil and the stirrup!

Hammer (Malleus)

Anvil (Incus)

Stirrup (Stapes)

KNOCK KNOCK!

WHO'S THERE?

EAR

EAR WHO?

EAR YOU ARE, I'VE BEEN LOOKING FOR YOU!

MORE THAN JUST HEARING

Ear This!

Not only are your ears used for hearing, but the inner ear also contains fluid that sends information to your brain about balance and movement.

Are We Nearly There Yet?

It's not just impatient people who yell this from the back seat of cars. Some people suffer from travel sickness, and really can't wait to get to their destination! Travel sickness can be brought on when you look out of a car window and your eyes tell your brain that you are moving. However, the fluid in your ears isn't moving and it tells your brain you are sitting still. Your brain gets confused and this sensation can make you feel sick!

You would also feel sick in the car if you had three pizzas, a milkshake, seven bananas, two cereal bars, five tuna sandwiches and a bunch of carrots just before you set off. Not that I've ever done that. Ever. Honestly.
Xand

FACT
The shape of your ears is as unique as your fingerprints!

In A Spin

The opposite effect happens if you spin around and suddenly stop. The fluid in your ears keeps moving, telling your brain that you are still spinning, but your eyes can see you have stopped. Again, your brain gets pretty confused and you feel a bit dizzy!

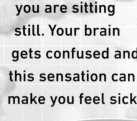

WHAT KIND OF EARS DO ENGINES HAVE?

I DON'T KNOW

ENGINEERS!

FACT
A man called Manjit Singh pulled a 7,400kg airliner along the ground for just under four metres, using his ears!

TOP TIP!
If you do suffer from travel sickness, try focusing on an object in the distance that isn't moving. Your eyes and ears will agree and send the same information to your brain, leaving it a little less confused!

SICK BAGS AT THE READY!

Xand had arranged for Chris to have a trip in a plane — complete with a slap-up lunch. Well, a tuna mayo sandwich.

Chris! Get a move on.
The plane is ready to take you on a little pleasure trip!

With a full belly, Chris was strapped in to the plane, excited to take to the skies for a nice relaxing flight.

Travelling at speeds of up to 250mph, Chris was having the time of his life. Look at that cheesy grin!

Pleased to be back on the ground, Chris managed to keep his tuna sandwich down. **Just.**

After a few loop-the-loops, and now flying upside down, Chris is not looking so happy! In fact, he's beginning to feel a bit sick ...

My little experiment worked! Just like when you feel sick in a car, there were so many different movements happening at such a high speed that Chris' eyes and ears were failing to send his brain the same messages at the same time. The only thing that would have made it better would have been if he'd actually thrown up!

Xand

FACT

The bits at the bottom of your outer ears are called earlobes. They may hang down (known as free earlobes) or be completely joined to the head (known as attached earlobes). Free earlobes are twice as common as attached ones!

WHAT TYPE DO YOU HAVE?

EAR'S the GROSS STUFF!

WAX FACTS!

Your body makes wax to stop things like dirt and water getting in to your inner ear. It takes about a month to travel from your inner ear to your outer ear. No wonder it tastes so revolting! *YUCK!*

FACT Earwax is actually a type of sweat!

FACT The ear contains the smallest bones in the body!

WAX ATTACKS!

Wax contains acid that deters bacteria, helping to keep infection out.

KEEP OUT!

OUCH! Take #41:

In the name of science, Xand tried some of his own earwax to find out what it tasted like! The result? It was quite a bitter flavour and not very nice at all. It's made up of around forty different substances, including fatty acids and cholesterol.

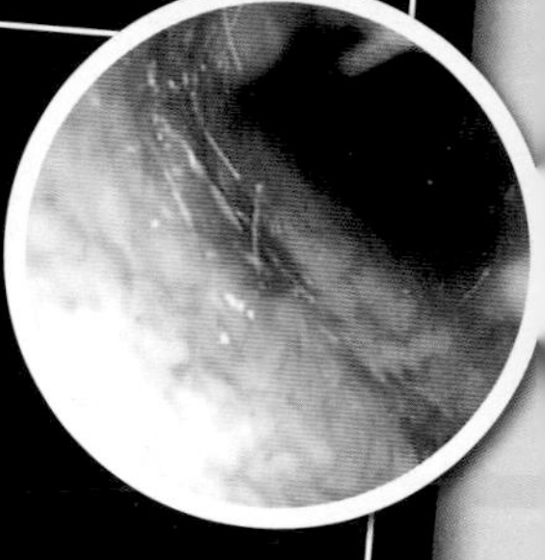

The things I do in the name of science so that YOU don't have to! Xand

FACT The cochlea contains about 20,000 sound-detecting hair cells!

I had glue ear when I was eight years old. The thick gloopy liquid was a bit like snot! Xand

GLOOPY GLUE!

Glue ear is a condition that affects about 80% of people before the age of ten, so if you're lucky enough not to have had it then someone else you know probably has! The main symptoms are hearing loss and ear ache. It is caused when a build-up of fluid, not wax, occurs around the ossicles and stops them from moving freely. Most of the time people grow out of glue ear without needing treatment, but in some cases a gadget called a 'grommet' needs to be fitted to drain the fluid.

DID YOU KNOW?

Most people take hearing for granted, but for some people who are deaf or hard of hearing, the world sounds like a very different place.

HEAR HEAR!

FACT

The ear canal is surrounded by a rigid tube called the temporal bone – one of the hardest bones in the human body!

Keep Out!

You should never put anything in your ear that's smaller than your own elbow! It's tempting to try to get your wax out, but can actually be very dangerous. If you're worried about wax, ask an adult to put a little olive oil in to soften it up, or check it out with your doctor.

Give Me a Sign

Some people use sign language and finger spelling. These methods of communication are based on shapes made with your fingers and hands.

I   LOVE   YOU

FACT

The older you get, the less you can hear. This is because the range of sounds you can detect narrows – and explains why you can probably hear more than your parents! (Unless you're deliberately ignoring them when they're telling you to tidy your room.)

Ear's Something Really Hi-Tech

OUCH! Take #3:

Xand met 12-year-old Matthew, who was having something called a cochlea Implant. Matthew's deafness was caused because the tiny hairs in his cochlea weren't working.

A cochlea implant is made up of two parts – a microphone, which hooks over the ear and hears what's going on . . .

. . . and a magnet that attaches through the skin. Little wires then go into the cochlea and send electric impulses to the brain.

DO TRY THIS AT HOME!

HERE'S A TRICK THAT CHRIS PLAYED ON XAND, AND YOU CAN TRY OUT ON YOUR FRIENDS AND FAMILY TOO!

Ask someone to sit on a chair in front of you, making sure that their back is against a wall. You need to make sure that their head is resting against the wall, and their hands are on their lap. Then, place your finger against their forehead and ask them to stand up.

THEY WON'T BE ABLE TO DO IT!

The reason why they can't stand up isn't because you've developed super-strength in your finger. It's because of their centre of gravity!

To be precise, it's to do with their balance. When you get up from a chair, you need to lean forward and shift your weight to your legs, adjusting your balance. If you can't lean forward, you can't stand up.

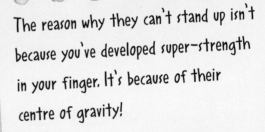

I still think my superior strength over my puny brother had something to do with it! Chris

Word sEARch

The word `ear` is in the word `search`, so we had to end this section with a word sEARch! See if you can find all these words. Good luck, **Ouch!** fans!

```
K E J F M D F M T V N H S B I
A Y B W D J W U K S G E T V A
L K K O S S Z R U H L D I T E
C O C H L E A D A C K V R H Z
W A X D R N B M I F E N R R Y
D G Y D E X M S Z E P D U D J
B N A P Y E S D U W R P P H U
Y A Y M R O N M A B B B C Q X Q
K X L W P E X D O I P X V S Y
T A M A Z T R P J K P T A E Z
V Z H C N B X D C S E U C A V
L L O M S C J N J A W F A R Q
I X B K J E E A N V I L K Q Q
G O J D X I D B E Y I T H B X
I U H E T B V S Z B F Y S D N
```

27

MOUTH TO MOUTH →

Multi-purpose Mouth!

There's a lot going on in your mouth –
tongue, teeth, taste-buds, throat, tonsils . . .

Do you think the person who named all the bits of the mouth loved the letter 't'? Xand

Taste's Good!

Your sense of taste works with your sense of
smell to help you identify the flavour of foods.
This explains why you can 'lose' your sense
of taste when you have a cold. You haven't
really lost anything, but because your nose is
blocked and you can't smell your food, your
brain isn't getting as many messages about
what you are eating.

Lips

XAND'S MOUTH

Teeth

Tongue

FACT
Your tongue print
is as unique as
your fingerprint!

Five Star Dining!

You can detect five
different tastes –
sweet, sour, salty,
bitter and umami.
Umami describes
strong savoury
flavours in
things like
cheese, meat
or fish.

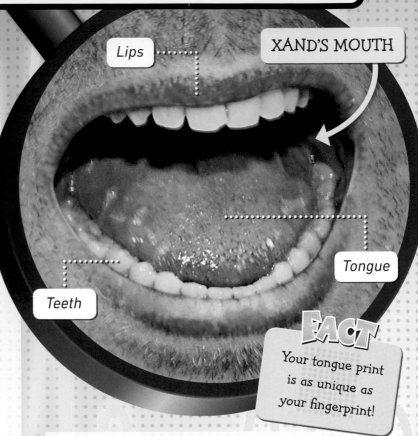

BITTER

SALTY

UMAMI

SALTY

SOUR

SOUR

SWEET

FACT
The tongue is covered in about 8,000
taste-buds, each containing up to 100 cells
helping you taste your food!

I Don't Like That!

Kids have more taste-buds than adults, so
you may be more sensitive to some bitter
foods. That's why kids often hate coffee and
Brussels sprouts!

Open Wide!

Your mouth is the gateway to two very important parts of your body. There are two tubes leading down from your throat – your windpipe (that goes to your lungs) and your oesophagus (that leads to your stomach). You might have heard the expression 'your food has gone down the wrong way'. This is when food ends up going down the wrong tube. It's not very nice when it happens, but your body makes you cough to get the food back up and send it down the right tube.

The Tooth of the Matter

Humans have twenty milk teeth, or baby teeth. These start falling out to make way for your adult teeth when you're about six or seven. Eventually, you'll have thirty-two adult teeth.

FACT

Despite what many think, the tongue isn't the strongest muscle. Check out page 52 to find out what is!

Lips

Palate

Tonsils

Epiglottis

Oesophagus

Hyoid

Teeth

Tongue

Windpipe

LUNGS THIS WAY

STOMACH THIS WAY

Imagine if this happened with other parts of your body like your arms or legs? Having parts of you fall off when you're young and new adult ones grow is quite strange when you think about it!

Chris

29

THE TOOTH, THE WHOLE TOOTH AND NOTHING BUT THE TOOTH

As well as giving you a beautiful smile, your teeth do lots of other things – they bite food into chunks, slice it, then chew it up and crush it into smaller bits ready to be swallowed.

WHAT DOES THE DENTIST OF THE YEAR GET?

I DON'T KNOW

A LITTLE PLAQUE!

Incisors

Canines

Molars

Premolars

Teeth Types

You have probably noticed that you have different types of teeth in your mouth, but do you know their names and what they do?

FACT

The average person spends 38.5 days of their life brushing their teeth.

INCISORS
You have eight chisel-like incisors at the front that slice your food

CANINES
There are four pointed canines that help to grip and tear

PREMOLARS
Your eight premolars are flat and grind and crush your food

MOLARS
These twelve teeth are similar in shape to the premolars and carry out the same job – grinding and crushing

Enamel

Gum

Pulp

Dentine

Jaw

Under the Surface

The surface of your teeth is made from enamel, the hardest material in the body. Beneath this is a bone-like structure called dentine. This goes down into your gum to form a root which holds your teeth in place in your jaw bone. Deeper down into your teeth is an area called the pulp – this contains blood vessels and nerves.

WHY DID THE QUEEN GO TO THE DENTIST?

I DON'T KNOW

TO GET A NEW CROWN!

THE TROUBLE WITH TEETH

YOU'VE PROBABLY BEEN TOLD THAT YOU SHOULD CLEAN YOUR TEETH REGULARLY. BUT IS IT REALLY THAT IMPORTANT? CHRIS AND XAND EMBARKED ON AN EXPERIMENT TO FIND OUT WHAT COULD HAPPEN IF YOU DON'T . . .

FACT
You are born with your milk teeth and your adult teeth already in your skull.

BEING THE, AHEM, WELL-BEHAVED ONE, I BRUSHED MY TEETH FOR TWO MINUTES IN THE MORNING AND TWO MINUTES BEFORE BED.

XAND HID MY TOOTHBRUSH, SO I WASN'T ABLE TO CLEAN MY TEETH AT ALL FOR TWO DAYS.

EVEN THOUGH MY TEETH FELT CLEAN, I SWILLED MY MOUTH WITH A SPECIAL BLUE LIQUID THAT SHOWS UP ANY PLAQUE. PLAQUE IS A MIXTURE OF FOOD PARTICLES, ACID AND BACTERIA THAT CAN ATTACK YOUR TEETH AND CAUSE DECAY.

PLAQUE

HAVING NOT BRUSHED THEM FOR TWO DAYS, MY TEETH FELT A BIT FUZZY – THAT WAS THE PLAQUE BEGINNING TO BUILD UP. I WASN'T LOOKING FORWARD TO SEEING THE RESULTS!

EVEN WITH CLEANING, THERE WERE STILL TRACES OF PLAQUE BEGINNING TO BUILD UP – YOU CAN SEE THEM HIGHLIGHTED IN THE DARK BLUE AREAS!

HOLY MOLARS! LOOK AT ALL THAT PLAQUE! THAT'S ALL POTENTIAL TOOTH DECAY WAITING TO HAPPEN. WHERE'S MY TOOTHBRUSH? XAND? XAND . . . ?

PLAQUE

FACT
You produce about 40,000 litres of spit in your lifetime. Or to put it another way, enough spit to fill around five hundred bathtubs – yuck!

WHAT DO YOU CALL A DENTIST WHO DOESN'T LIKE TEA?

I DON'T KNOW

DENIS

FACT
Most people have 32 adult teeth. The world record is held by a man in India who has 37!

Tongue Tied

YOUR TONGUE PLAYS A MAJOR ROLE IN GETTING FOOD FROM YOUR MOUTH TO YOUR STOMACH. IT'S TIME TO GO ON A JOURNEY!

FIRST STOP
The rough surface of your tongue helps to position your food in the correct part of your mouth for your teeth to chew it.

NEXT!
Your tongue also helps mix food with saliva from the salivary glands ready for swallowing.

JUST CHECKING!
Your tongue's taste-buds work out the flavour of the food you're eating, and send messages to your brain.

GOING DOWN!
Your tongue can detect when it's time to send your food down your throat for processing in the stomach.

MOVE ALONG PLEASE!
The rather clever epiglottis is a movable flap that makes sure food goes down your oesophagus and into your stomach by covering up your trachea* that leads to your lungs. Something you almost definitely don't know about the epiglottis is that it's Chris and Xand's favourite body part!

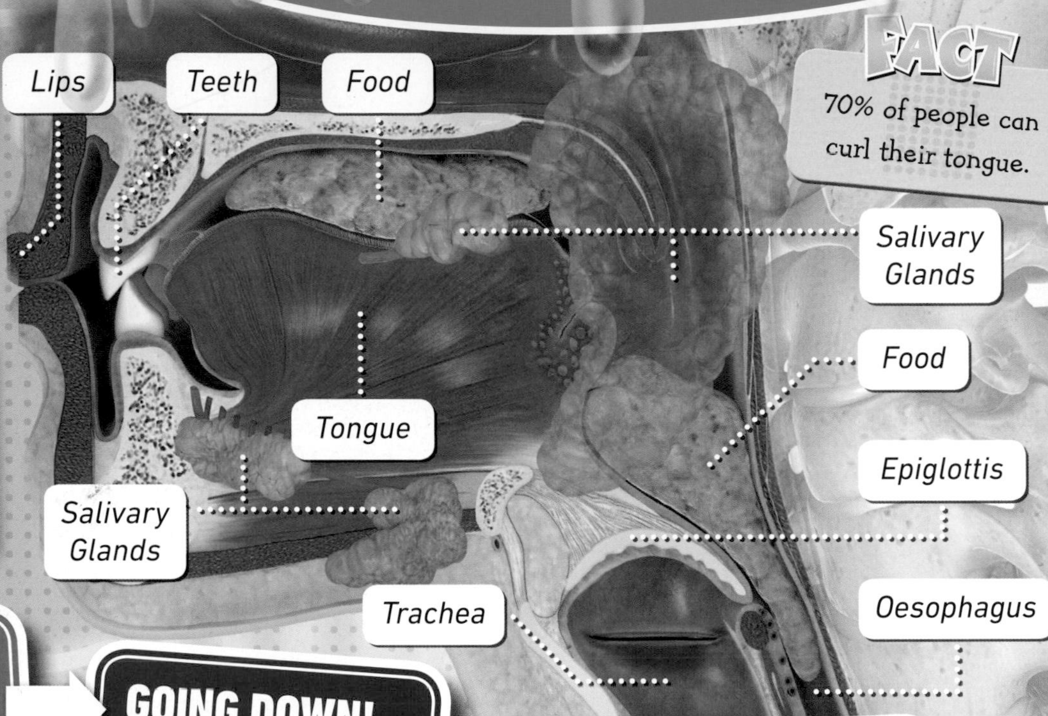

*Also known as your windpipe, fact fans! Chris

FACT
70% of people can curl their tongue.

Lips   Teeth   Food

Salivary Glands

Food

Tongue

Epiglottis

Salivary Glands

Oesophagus

Trachea

OUCH! Take #619:

Chris and Xand met a man with a tongue. A long tongue. A very long tongue. Stephen Taylor's tongue is an incredible 10cm long from his tongue tip to his lip! That's as long as a sausage!

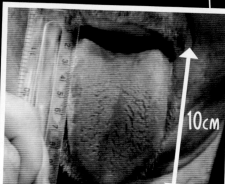

10CM

NON-MEDICAL FACT: your tongue is also useful for sticking out at your twin brother when he annoys you! Xand

WHAT TIME DO MOST PEOPLE GO TO THE DENTIST?

I DON'T KNOW

TOOTH HURTY

EH?

TOOTH HURTY, AS IN 2.30, GET IT? HONESTLY, MY HUMOUR IS WASTED ON YOU ...

DO TRY THIS AT HOME!

TIME FOR A TANTALIZING TONGUE TWISTING TASTE-TESTER TO TRY!

1. First you will need to find someone who is willing to lend you their tongue in the name of medical science. But tell them not to worry — their tongue will remain attached to their body at all times!

FACT
The inside of your mouth hosts about as many bacteria as there are people on Earth.

2. Next, you'll need to make sure that the tongue is really dry — paper towel or kitchen roll works really well.

3. Place a small piece of food on their tongue. Chocolate works well.

4. Ask them to guess what food is on their tongue.

FACT
Some mouth bacteria are good and actually secrete enzymes to fight bad bacteria.

5. Chances are, they won't be able to taste the food!

6. Tell them to start chewing and they should be able to identify the food pretty quickly. This demonstrates that in order for your mouth to be able to taste the food, the food must be dissolved in saliva first, and only then can the flavour be detected by your taste-buds.

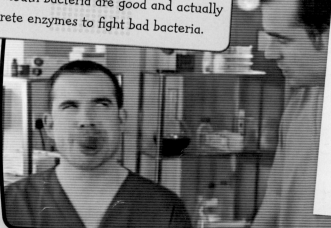

33

Malfunctioning Mouths

WITH SO MUCH GOING ON, IT'S NOT SURPRISING THAT QUITE A LOT CAN GO WRONG INSIDE YOUR MOUTH. SAY 'AAAAAHH!' . . .

Tooth ....

ABSCESS

Mouth Ulcers

FACT
Two thirds of each tooth are hidden under the gum.

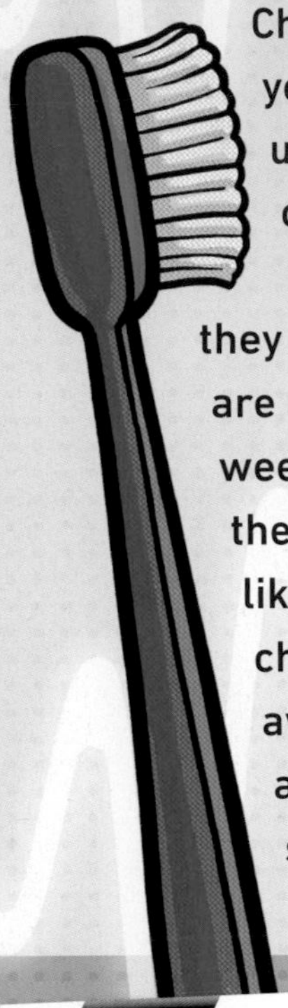

Chances are, you'll suffer from a mouth ulcer at some point as they're pretty common. They are painful sores that appear in your mouth. Although they can be very uncomfortable, they are usually harmless and go within a week or two. If you're feeling impatient, there are some things you could try like switching to a softer toothbrush, changing your toothpaste, and avoiding food that is hard, spicy, salty, acidic or hot. You could even try sipping a cool drink through a straw.

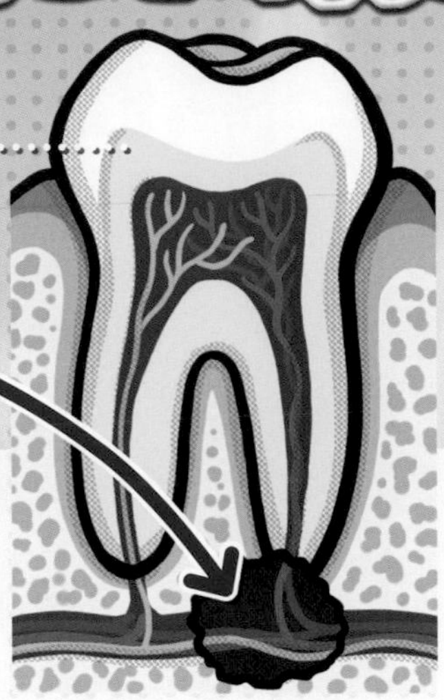

Dental Abscess

A dental abscess happens when yucky pus forms inside the teeth, in the gums, or in the bone that holds the teeth in place, and is caused by a bacterial infection. It can be particularly painful and you should definitely see a dentist to get treatment because they won't go away on their own and can actually spread to other parts of the body and make you very unwell.

Tonsil Trouble

FACT
Right-handed people tend to chew on the right side of their mouth, and left-handed people on the left side.

OUCH! Take #51:

Like lots of people, when Xand was younger, he had his tonsils removed because he had an infection. Fast forward to when he was filming *Operation Ouch!* and Xand met Dr Anand Kasbekar who specializes in everything to do with your ear, nose and throat. Xand found out that although we don't entirely know what your tonsils do, we think that they help fight infection. And thankfully, we can function quite happily without them – phew!

This is what one of Dr Anand's patients' tonsils looked like inside their mouth ...

TONSILS

... and this is them once they were removed!

TONSILS

34

Tongue Twisters

IT'S TIME TO GIVE YOUR TONGUE A WORKOUT! SEE HOW QUICKLY YOU CAN SAY THESE TONGUE TWISTERS OUT LOUD!

1. If two witches were watching two watches, which witch would watch which watch?

2. The big bug bit the little beetle, but the little beetle bit the big bug back.

3. I can think of six thin things, but I can think of six thick things too.

4. Fresh fried fish, fish fresh fried, fried fish fresh, fish fried fresh.

5. A thousand tricky tongue twisters trip thrillingly off the tongue.

KNOW YOUR NOSE →

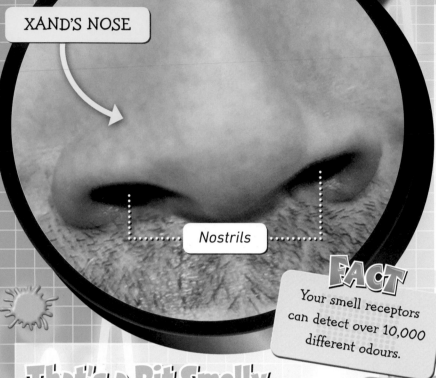

XAND'S NOSE

Nostrils

Let's Get Nosey!

This is Xand's nose. It's a lot like Chris' nose. And, come to think of it, it's probably a lot like your nose too. There is the bit that sticks out from your face, and at the bottom are two holes called nostrils. The shape of your nose depends on the shape of your nasal bone and nasal cartilage (which is just a kind of flexible body tissue).

FACT
Your smell receptors can detect over 10,000 different odours.

What Does It Do?

You breathe air in to your lungs through your nose. Or at least that's the simple explanation. Your nose works a bit like an air-conditioning system that actually warms, filters and moistens the air before it reaches your lungs. There are also tiny little hairs in your nose that act as a line of defence to stop things like dust getting into your lungs.

That's a Bit Smelly

The nostrils are openings that allow smells and odours to enter the body for our brain to process and decide whether it's a smell we like or don't.

'Snot Just For Picking

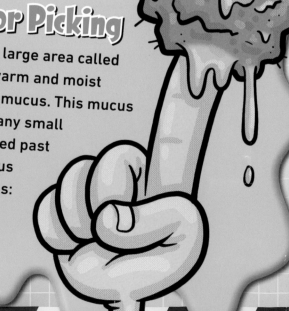

Behind your nostrils is a large area called your nasal cavity. It's a warm and moist place, lined with a sticky mucus. This mucus helps to trap germs and any small particles that have sneaked past the hairs. This nasal mucus has lots of different names: bogies, snot, boogers . . . What do you call yours?

Xand's stinky PE kit is definitely an example of a bad smell. Believe me, I smelt it once. Never, ever again! Chris

Who Nose What They Do!

Around your nasal cavity are air-filled spaces called your sinuses. Although this book is supposed to tell you how your body works, the truth is, no one really knows what your sinuses do. Some people think that they control body temperature, while others think that they are there to make your skull lighter. What we all agree on, though, is that blocked sinuses are not much fun. Yours may have been blocked when you have had a cold. They can make it hard to breathe, and don't even get us started on the amount of snot that they let leak out of your nose . . .

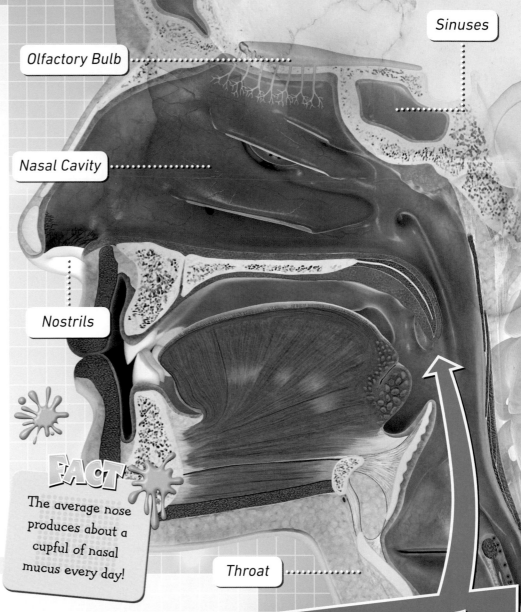

Olfactory Bulb

Sinuses

Nasal Cavity

Nostrils

Throat

FACT
The average nose produces about a cupful of nasal mucus every day!

Wow!

About 7cm up your nose is a thing called the olfactory bulb. It's not an actual factory (despite its name), but it does have a very important job. Smells reach it through the nostrils, and then tiny hairs called cilia process the smells by dissolving odour molecules in a mucus and then sending signals to the brain, where individual smells are identified.

Working Together

From the outside, your nose, ears and mouth might appear to be very separate, but when you get inside, you realize that they are connected to each other!

FACT
Humans have about 40 million smell-detecting cilia in the olfactory system!

Two-Way Traffic

IT'S NOT ONLY AIR AND SMELLS THAT GO UP OUR NOSES. OCCASIONALLY STUFF COMES DOWN TOO!

BRILLIANT!
This is going to be the section on snot — my favourite! Chris

READY SALTED

You've probably never eaten a bogey, have you? Which means you have no idea what they taste of. So, in case you were wondering whether they taste of strawberries, or chocolate brownies, or roast chicken, we can put you out of your misery. Bogies actually taste quite salty, which makes sense because salt is one of the 'ingredients' in your snot.

Might need to rethink the snot restaurant menu — there might not be enough variety! Xand

FACT
Sneezes travel at up to 100mph!

BELIEVE IT OR SNOT...

You might want to be sitting down for this fact, but you don't sneeze through your nose. Crazy, right? When you sneeze, you actually spray saliva from your mouth. This is then sometimes followed by nasal mucus running down your nose. It does this to help flush out whatever caused the sneeze in the first place.

This is why it's a good idea to cover your nose AND your mouth when you sneeze!
Chris

IT'S SNOT ART

If you sneeze when you're unwell, every single one of those droplets that comes out could contain disease-spreading germs and that's why it's so important to cover your mouth. To demonstrate how powerful a sneeze can be, Chris and Xand drank coloured liquids and then sneezed. The results were snot artistic!

PLEASE DON'T TRY THIS AT HOME, it's snot big and it's snot clever. You'd end up making a mess and then we'd get in all sorts of bother! Chris

SICK? SOT? SICKY SNOT?

Your nose, mouth and stomach are all connected and this is why sometimes sick can end up coming out of your mouth and nose at the same time! Unfortunately, no one has come up with a name for sick that comes out your nose yet, so it's up to you what you call it!

OUCH! Take #49:

Did you know that the colour of your snot can reveal a lot about you? If it's clear, you're probably quite healthy, whereas if it's a yellowy-green colour, you probably have an infection. But more than that, experts can use your snot to find out about where you live. Chris met up with Dr Kelly Berube who was able to tell that he lived in a big city from the soot particles she could see. She also identified some pollen mixed in with Chris' snot too, meaning his nasal mucus was doing a great job of keeping stuff out.

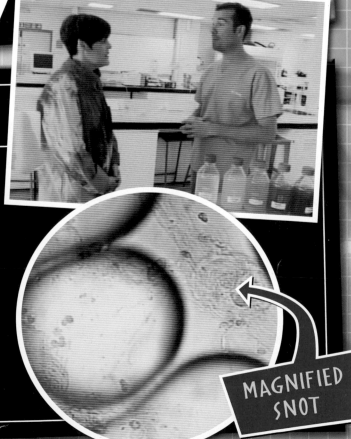

MAGNIFIED SNOT

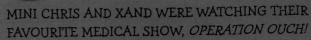

MINI Chris + Xand

MUM NOSE BEST

MINI CHRIS AND XAND WERE WATCHING THEIR FAVOURITE MEDICAL SHOW, *OPERATION OUCH!*

STOP PICKING YOUR NOSE, IT'S DISGUSTING!

BUT THERE'S JUST ONE MORE BOGEY I NEED TO GET

MINI CHRIS LOOKS AT MINI XAND AND NOTICES SOMETHING ...

ER, XAND, DON'T PANIC, BUT THERE'S BLOOD DRIPPING FROM YOUR NOSE!

MUUMMM!

MINI CHRIS AND MINI XAND ARE IN TROUBLE NOW!

HAVE YOU TWO BEEN FIGHTING AGAIN?

NO, MUM!

WE WERE WATCHING TV AND I WAS JUST PICKING MY NOSE!

NOT AGAIN!

I WANT YOU TO SIT DOWN QUIETLY AND FIRMLY PINCH THE SOFT PART OF YOUR NOSE.

WHAT'S WRONG WITH HIM?

IT'S AN EPISTAXIS.

AN EPI-WHAT?

OTHERWISE KNOWN AS A NOSEBLEED, PROBABLY BROUGHT ON BY YOUR EXCESSIVE NOSE PICKING.

I DON'T KNOW WHY YOU DO IT. MINI CHRIS DOESN'T!

CAN I STOP THIS YET?

MUM SAID 10–15 MINUTES, AND DON'T FORGET, MUM NOSE BEST!

If you get a nosebleed, always tell a grown-up!

Tasty!

Brain

Olfactory Bulb

Smell Receptors

Taste-buds

Wow!

Did you know that you don't just taste with your mouth? Your nose has an important role to play too . . .

Guess what?

As you discovered on pages 28 and 29 of your HuManual, your taste-buds are located on your tongue. However, as you now know, all they can 'taste' is whether a food is sweet, sour, salty, bitter or umami. It is only when your saliva starts to dissolve your food and sends messages to the brain about it that flavours can be identified . . .

FACT
Your nostrils are separated by something called your nasal septum.

Amazing

So, whilst your mouth is busy with your food, millions of smell receptors that are located in your nasal cavity are busy sending signals to your brain where individual smells are identified. Your tongue and nose are the perfect team – a bit like Chris and Xand!

Brain power

Your brain analyses all the information sent to it from the taste-buds and the smell receptors in your nasal cavity. It then signals for saliva and stomach juices to get ready for digestion of the food.

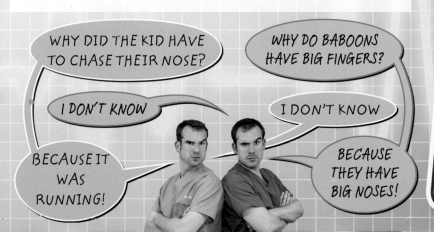

WHY DID THE KID HAVE TO CHASE THEIR NOSE?

WHY DO BABOONS HAVE BIG FINGERS?

I DON'T KNOW

I DON'T KNOW

BECAUSE IT WAS RUNNING!

BECAUSE THEY HAVE BIG NOSES!

⚠ DANGER! ⚠

You've probably experienced when your sense of smell has warned your body about food that might be going off or bad – it generally smells pretty disgusting and you naturally don't want to eat it when you get a whiff of it. In doing this, your nose helps you to avoid becoming poorly or unwell.

DO TRY THIS AT HOME!

HERE'S ONE FOR YOUR FAMILY AND FRIENDS WHO LIKE TO THINK OF THEMSELVES AS FOODIES . . .

1. First, you need to find someone who likes yogurt.

2. Then you need to get hold of three different flavours of yogurt and cover up the label (or put them into three different dishes).

3. Next, feed a spoonful of each one to your taste tester and ask them to identify the flavour. They should find this quite easy.

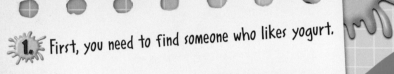

NOW, TO DEMONSTRATE THE ROLE THAT YOUR NOSE PLAYS IN HOW WE TASTE THINGS . . .

4. Ask your taste tester to close or cover their eyes. When they've done this, switch round the yogurts.

5. Then, ask them to pinch their nose.

6. Now, feed them a spoonful of each one again and see if they can work out the flavours. Chances are, they won't be able to do it!

The science bit!

Whenever we eat or drink something, our senses of smell and taste work together. Without being able to smell our food, it can taste a bit bland and boring – just like when your nose is blocked up with a cold.

THE SMELLING TEST

1. What is the name of the flexible body tissue that helps give your nose its shape?

A. nasal cartridge   B. nasal carthorse   C. nasal cartilage

2. How fast does a sneeze travel?

A. 10mph   B. 100mph   C. 1,000mph

3. What are the air-filled cavities in your nasal passage called?

A. sinuses   B. no uses   C. confuses

4. Where do sneezes come from?

A. your mouth   B. your nose   C. your ears

5. What do most bogeys taste like?

A. sweet   B. spicy   C. salty

6. How many odours can your smell receptors detect?

A. about 1,000   B. about 10,000   C. about 100,000

7. How far up your nose is your olfactory bulb?

A. about 2cm   B. about 7cm   C. about 20cm

8. It is the job of the cilia in the olfactory system to detect smells, but how many cilia are there?

A. about 40,000   B. about 4 million   C. about 40 million

9. How much nasal mucus do you produce on average each day?

A. a teaspoon   B. a cup   C. a barrel

10. Which of these was found in Chris' snot?

A. flour   B. soot   C. sand

THE BARE BONES →

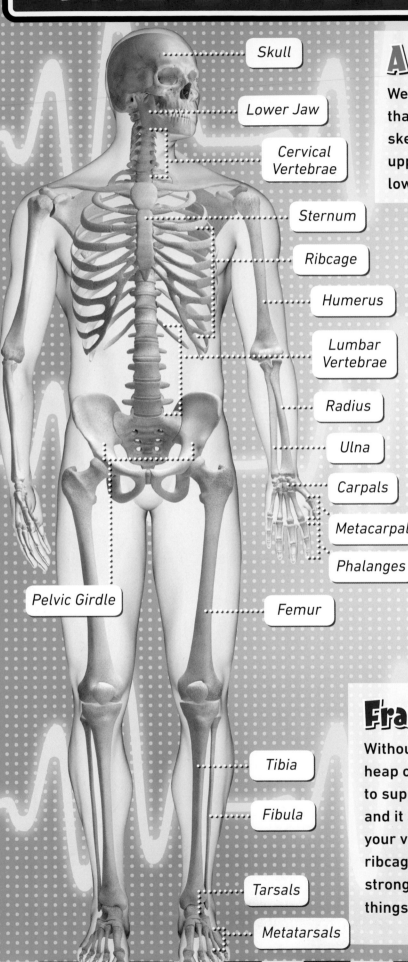

Skull

Lower Jaw

Cervical Vertebrae

Sternum

Ribcage

Humerus

Lumbar Vertebrae

Radius

Ulna

Carpals

Metacarpals

Phalanges

Pelvic Girdle

Femur

Tibia

Fibula

Tarsals

Metatarsals

A Bone to Pick with You!

Well actually, 206 bones to pick with you – because that's the number of bones that make up the human skeleton! They include your collarbone, breastbone, upper arms, forearms, ribs, hip bone, thigh bone, lower leg bones . . . the list goes on!

When Is a Bone Not a Bone?

Your arm has three bones – the ulna, radius and humerus. If you've ever banged your elbow, you may have got a tingly sensation, which is why some people call it your funny bone. Although technically you've actually hit your ulnar nerve, which isn't a bone at all!

So let's get this right. Your funny bone isn't funny and isn't a bone? Someone needs to have a word with trading standards! Xand

Framework

Without your skeleton, your body would collapse in a heap on the floor. Your skeleton provides a framework to support you and shape you, and it also helps protect your vital organs. Your ribcage is particularly strong and guards things like your heart.

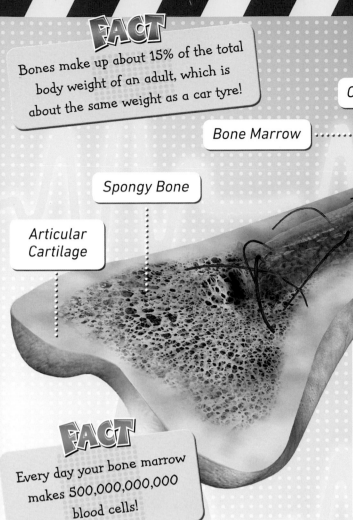

Periosteum

Compact Bone

Bone Marrow

Spongy Bone

Articular Cartilage

Blood Vessels

Time to Bone Up on Bones!

Bones are living things with lots going on inside. They are incredibly strong, but also very light because the dense heavy tissue is only on the outside. Bones don't only hold your body up, they are also like little factories that make blood cells and store calcium.

Throw a Doc a Bone . . .

. . . and they're sure to saw it open to have a look inside! Starting from the outside, you'll find a layer of dense bone. Beneath this is a much lighter layer of spongy bone. In the middle of the bone you'll find a central cavity filled with bone marrow. The whole thing is covered in a membrane called the periosteum.

The Marrow Machine

Bone marrow plays a very important role because it is here that your body makes red blood cells. When you are growing, you need more red blood cells, so your bone marrow will be more pinky red than that of an adult because of the number of red cells the bone marrow is producing. As you get older, bone marrow becomes more creamy yellow. This is because it becomes a place to store fat.

Hi! My name is Marrow!

WHAT IS THE MOST MUSICAL BONE?

I DON'T KNOW

THE TROM-BONE!

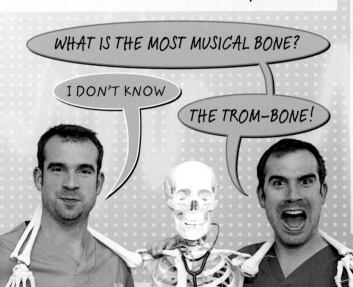

You'll have to just trust us on this one as hopefully you'll never get to see your own bone marrow! Chris

The Skull

FACT
There is a big hole in the base of your skull called the foramen magnum. The brain stem goes through it to meet the spinal cord.

Protection

Perhaps the most impressive part of your skeleton is the skull. It's a bit like the housing of a computer, laptop or tablet, protecting the important and delicate bits inside, except instead of circuit boards and processors, your skull protects your brain, eyes and ears.

Structure

Your skull also determines the shape of your face and head – although you might not recognize your own skull in an identity parade!

I'm sure I'd recognize my skull if it was next to Chris' – mine would be the better-looking one!   Xand

How Many Bones?

The skull contains not one, but an amazing 22 bones! And all but one of them are fixed in place. Your lower jaw is able to move, which is pretty cool because if it didn't you wouldn't be able to eat, drink, talk, sing or yawn when you're in a boring class at school! The other 21 bones are locked together by immovable joints called sutures that look like a zig-zaggy puzzle.

Sutures

Face Forwards!

The front of your skull contains bones that support your face (your facial bones), whereas the ones at the top, back and sides protect your brain (your cranial bones).

FACT
In the 19th century, people called phrenologists thought they could work out people's characters from little bumps on their skulls.

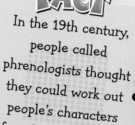

WHAT DO SKELETONS SAY BEFORE EATING?

I DON'T KNOW

BONE APPETIT!

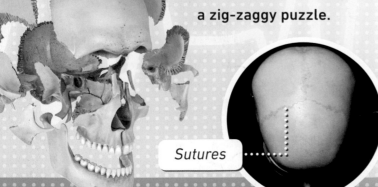

No 'Arm Done

FACT
Bones are made up of calcium, phosphorus, sodium and other minerals, as well as a protein called collagen.

Frac Facts

A break or a crack in a bone is called a fracture. Breaks that don't damage any of the surrounding tissue are called clean fractures, whereas ones that do damage the tissue or break through the skin are called compound fractures.

Clean Fracture | *Compound Fracture*

X-ray Vision

It's not just superheroes like Superman who have X-ray vision– doctors do too! They use a special piece of kit to take a kind of photograph to see what's going on and find out if you have a fracture. If they find one, they may need to push the bone back into position before applying a plaster cast to keep it in place.

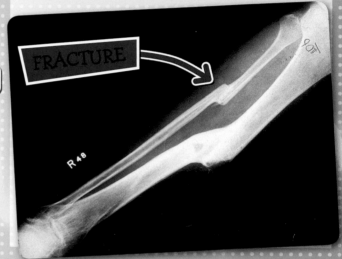

FRACTURE

R 48

Self-healing

Bones have the pretty cool ability to heal themselves, but this can take weeks or months depending on how bad the fracture is and what bone you've broken.

FACT
Arms are among the most commonly broken bones, accounting for almost half of all adults' broken bones. The collarbone is the most commonly broken bone among children.

Dislocation, Dislocation, Dislocation

When you dislocate something like your thumb, you don't break it, but the bones are forced out of line. Ouch! You'll need to see a doctor who will force the bone back into the correct position.

DOUBLE OUCH!

WHO WAS THE MOST FAMOUS SKELETON DETECTIVE?

I DON'T KNOW

SHERLOCK BONES!

I HOPE YOU FIND THIS BONE JOKE HUMERUS

Chilled to the Bone

THIS MIGHT LOOK LIKE A FIELD OF SNOWMEN, BUT ONE OF THEM HAS A SKULL FOR A HEAD — CAN YOU FIND IT?

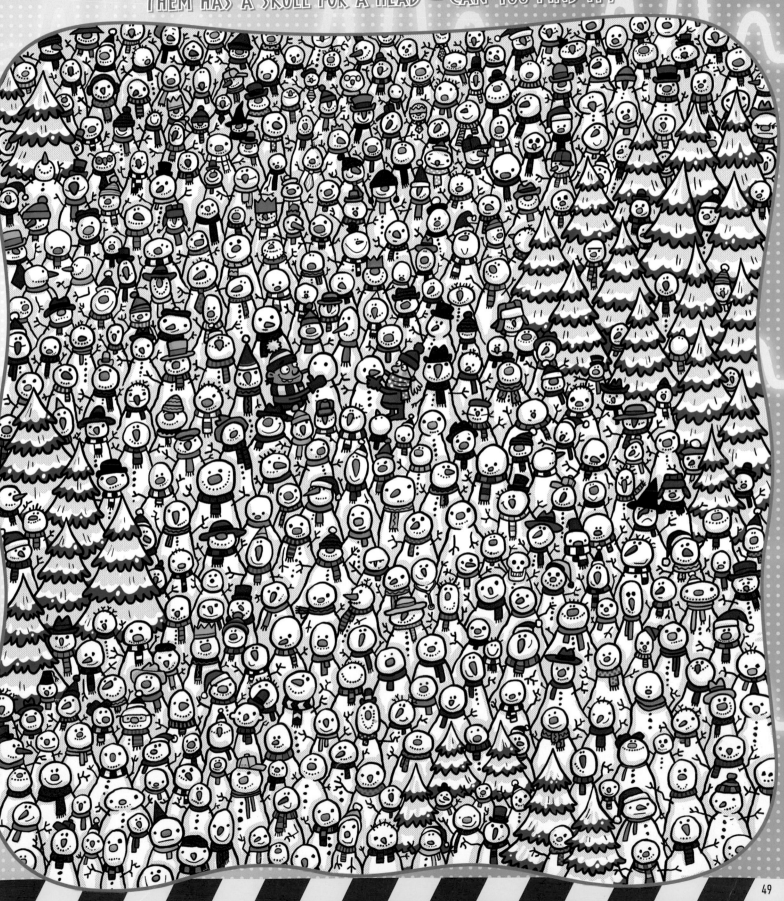

Flexible Friends

BONES ARE HELD TOGETHER BY THINGS CALLED JOINTS — THEY ARE WHAT ALLOWS YOU TO MOVE AROUND AND BE FLEXIBLE.

Your body contains about 350 joints. Some connect two bones, whereas others join several together.

You are about 1cm taller in the morning when you first get up than when you go to bed. This is because during the day the soft cartilage between your bones gets squashed and compressed.

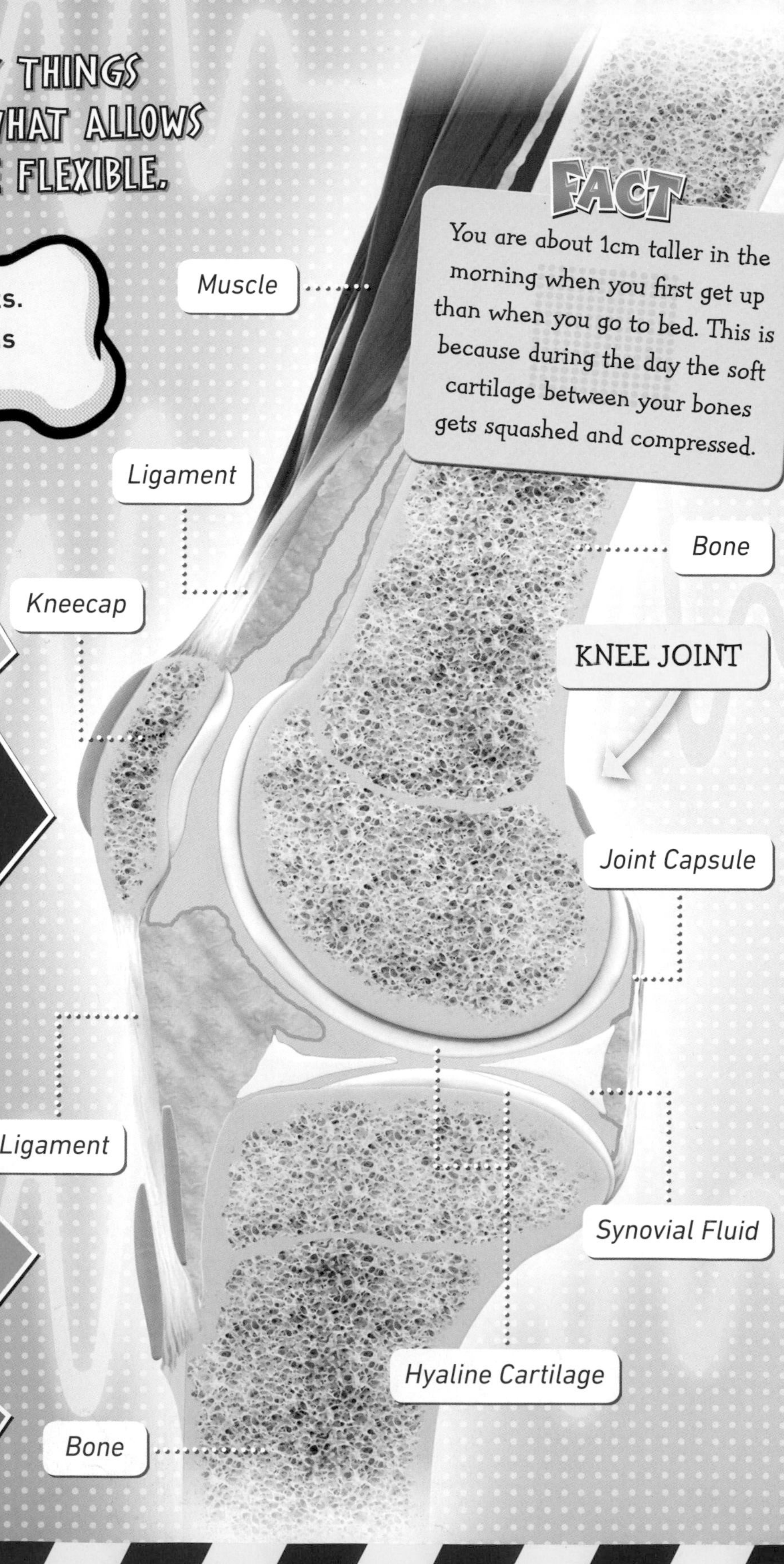

Muscle

Ligament

Bone

Kneecap

KNEE JOINT

- THIS KNEE JOINT SHOWS WHAT IS GOING ON UNDER THE SKIN

- THE END OF EACH BONE IS CAPPED WITH HYALINE CARTILAGE TO REDUCE FRICTION AT THE JOINTS

Joint Capsule

- THE OILY SYNOVIAL FLUID FILLS THE SPACE BETWEEN THE TWO BONES AND MAKES THE CARTILAGE SLIPPERY SO THAT IT CAN MOVE EASILY

Ligament

Synovial Fluid

- EVERYTHING IS HELD TOGETHER IN A JOINT CAPSULE

Hyaline Cartilage

- LIGAMENTS ARE THERE TO REINFORCE THE JOINT

Bone

THERE ARE SIX BASIC TYPES OF JOINT IN YOUR BODY —
LET'S FIND OUT HOW THEY WORK AND WHERE THEY ARE USED:

NAME: **Pivot joint**

MOVEMENT: **Swivel**

EXAMPLE: **Shaking your head to say 'no'**

NAME: **Hinge joint**

MOVEMENT: **One direction only**

EXAMPLE: **Elbows, fingers**

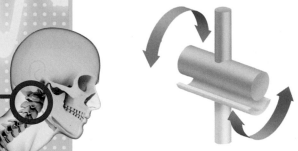

NAME: **Ball-and-socket joint**

MOVEMENT: **Rotation**

EXAMPLE: **Shoulders and hips**

NAME: **Ellipsoidal joint**

MOVEMENT: **Side to side or backwards and forwards**

EXAMPLE: **Base of fingers and toes**

NAME: **Saddle joint**

MOVEMENT: **Considerable sweeping mobility**

EXAMPLE: **Base of thumb**

WHY DID THE SKELETON LAUGH?

I DON'T KNOW

BECAUSE SOMEONE TICKLED HIS FUNNY BONE!

NAME: **Plane joint**

MOVEMENT: **Limited side-to-side gliding**

EXAMPLE: **Wrist and ankle bones**

MUSCLE POWER →

Which reminds me, I must go down to the gym. I'll just read a bit more of this HuManual first... Xand

Fascicle

Muscle Fibre

Myofibril

Hard Workers

Muscles help us do all sorts of things like lift heavy objects, run super-fast and jump up really high. However, they also help us do more normal things like talk, eat and breathe. Just picking up this book required the muscles in your fingers, hands, wrists, arms, shoulders, eyes, head and neck to work together.

FACT

There are three types of muscle: skeletal, cardiac and smooth.

Smile!

The muscles in our faces help us make all sorts of expressions and can let other people know whether we are happy, sad, angry or just a bit confused.

FACT

The masseter muscle in your jaw is the strongest in the body for its size.

Thin Filament

Thick Filament

This is what the inside of a muscle fibre looks like – it's filled with rod-like myofibrils, each containing thick and thin filaments. When a muscle contracts, the filaments interact and slide over each other to make the muscle shorter.

OUCH! Take #876:

Chris and Xand met a man called Tiny. Everyone's muscles are made up of fibres formed of millions of individual cells and blood vessels that deliver the energy that your muscles need in order to move. Each individual muscle fibre on its own isn't very strong but when you gather a bunch of them together they become much more powerful. When Tiny goes to the gym and lifts weights, he causes small tears in the muscle fibres and that in turn stimulates his body to build those fibres back bigger and stronger than before.

Working Together

Muscles work by pulling parts of your body, but they can't push. This is why they are often arranged in pairs that do opposing work – when one is pulling, the other one is relaxing. This happens in your arm. When the bicep does its thing, it shortens and pulls your arm up. And then when your tricep gets to work, it shortens and pulls your lower arm down.

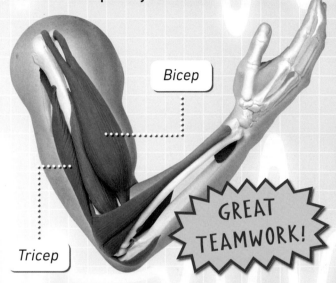

Bicep

Tricep

GREAT TEAMWORK!

FACT

The word muscle comes from the Latin 'musculus', which means 'little mouse'. Some people have said that this could be because muscles moving under the skin look like mice moving under a rug!

WANT TO KNOW WHAT MAKES ME SMILE?

WHAT?

MY FACE MUSCLES!

OUCH! Take #5:

To make your muscles move, your brain sends a message in the form of a small electrical charge down your nerves to your muscle. In the lab, Xand decided to do the work of Chris' brain and send electrical messages to Chris' muscles by attaching electricity-conducting pads to his arms. The results got a bit messy!

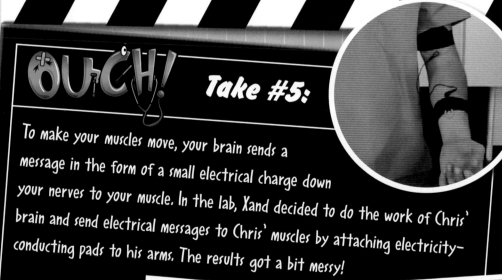

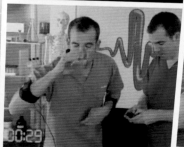

53

DO TRY THIS AT HOME!

HERE'S A MUSCLE TRICK TO TRY OUT ON YOUR FRIENDS . . .

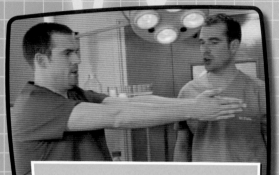

1. Ask your friend to put their arms out in front of them.

2. Then tell them to rub their left elbow with their right hand for about 30 seconds, whilst you say the magic arm-shortening spell 'Arm-bra cadabra!'

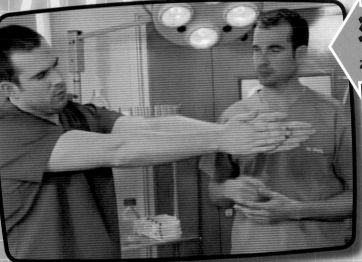

3. Then tell them to put their right arm out in front of them and they'll discover that it looks shorter than the left one!

4. You can then tell them that if they want to get their arms back to being the same length, they should rub their right elbow with their left hand, and then hold their arms out in front of them again.

FACT

The biggest muscle in your body is in your bum and it's called the gluteus maximus.

FACT

The smallest muscle, the stapedius, is just over 1mm long and is in your ear.

5. This trick works because as you rub your left elbow, the muscles in your right shoulder tighten up, making your right arm look shorter – your left arm is relaxed and completely untensed, so it looks longer.

FACT

Throwing a ball uses almost all of your 600 muscles.

Wow!

Lots of us take walking for granted, but did you know that walking uses around 200 muscles?

FACT

Walking sideways burns 78% more calories than walking forward.

Great! So does that mean that if I walk sideways, I can have 78% more lunch? Xand

In Style!

The basic action of walking is almost the same for everyone, placing one foot in front of the other. But did you know that everyone has their own individual style of walking? This is called their 'gait'.

FACT

The average baby starts walking at 13 months old.

Not to be confused with a school gate or a garden gate. Those have nothing to do with the way you walk! Chris

Clever Stuff!

Xand visited the Gait Lab at Alder Hey Hospital in Liverpool. By attaching clever sensors and using cameras, they were able to assess how people walk. When Xand had a go he discovered that he had quite a normal walk. That was until they made him put on a pair of high-heel shoes!

FACT

If you walked for 12 hours a day, it would take the average person 690 days to walk around the world.

Think I'll stick to my regular footwear! Xand

The computer revealed that Xand didn't ever straighten his knees when walking in high heels. Doing this over a long period of time could lead to all sorts of problems with your feet, knees, hips and back.

Sprains & Strains

Ouch!

With everything they do, it's not surprising that sprains and strains are very common injuries that affect muscles and ligaments. You might injure yourself when playing sport, fall over or bash into someone or something.

Sprain Pain

A sprain happens when your ligaments (tissue that holds your bones together) get stretched or twisted. The most common sprains include knees, ankles, wrists and thumbs.

FACT
Muscles make up about 40% of your body weight.

SWOLLEN ANKLE

Take the Strain

A muscle strain is caused when a muscle is pulled so hard that some of the fibres get damaged. In extreme cases, the fibres can stretch so much they break, which is known as a torn muscle – and it's as painful as it sounds! Muscle strains are particularly common in the legs and back. You may have heard of footballers straining their hamstrings – depending on how bad the injury is, they can be out of action for days, weeks or even months!

FACT
The only muscle that never tires is the heart.

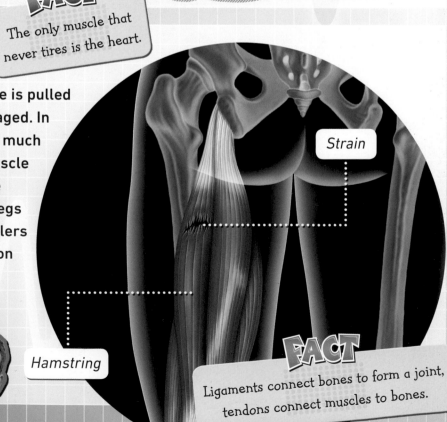
Strain

Hamstring

FACT
Ligaments connect bones to form a joint, tendons connect muscles to bones.

Well at least they can use that time to watch lots of episodes of Operation Ouch! Chris

Let's Get Physical

OUCH! Take #88:

Chris and Xand met John who is a footballing genius! He's a maestro at pulling off tricks and flicks. This keepy-uppy king trains more than forty hours a week and has even completed the London Marathon while keeping the ball in the air. This is all possible because the part of the brain called the motor cortex is working with John's muscles and telling them what to do. Oh, and a LOT of practice!

FACT
Taking just one step uses about 200 muscles.

DON'T TRY THIS AT HOME!

OUCH! Take #720:

This is Delia Du Sol. And yes, she is in a plastic box! Delia is a contortionist and is able to bend her body and squeeze into very small spaces. Inside Delia's limbs she has super-stretchy ligaments — that's the soft tissue that holds our bones together. Although she was born this way, Delia trains hard every day to make sure her ligaments remain flexible. Who knows, she might even go to a special contortionists school, so please, please don't try this yourself at home.

OUCH! Take #67:

Meet Tim 'Livewire' Shieff. He's a free runner and this is him demonstrating the human flag. This move requires extreme control of his abdominal and lateral muscles to raise his legs high in the air. Now that's amazing.

FACT
There are more than fifty muscles in your face.

DO TRY THIS AT HOME!

YOUR JOINTS WORK VERY HARD A LOT OF THE TIME. BUT HERE'S A WAY TO TRICK YOUR FRIENDS' JOINTS INTO RELAXING SO MUCH THEY WILL THINK THAT THEY ARE FALLING THROUGH THE FLOOR!

1. Get a friend to lie on the floor with their arms out to the sides and their eyes closed.

2. Then lift their feet up to about your waist height.

3. Very slowly lower their feet towards the ground, asking them to guess how close to the floor they are.

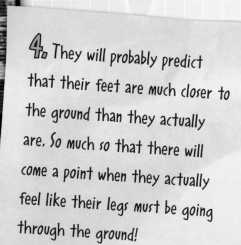

4. They will probably predict that their feet are much closer to the ground than they actually are, So much so that there will come a point when they actually feel like their legs must be going through the ground!

The science bit!

This happens because when their legs are held up in the air, the nerves in your friend's joints relax and stop telling their brain where their legs are. Keeping their eyes closed further confuses their brain as they try to work out the position of their legs. Their brain keeps getting it wrong, leading to the sensation (known as proprioception) that their legs are actually falling through the floor!

Muscle or Mussel?

The muscles in your body have some pretty cool scientific names, but so do the mussels that live in the sea!

CAN YOU GUESS WHICH OF THESE ARE MUSCLES IN YOUR BODY, AND WHICH ONES ARE MUSSELS THAT LIVE IN WATER? GIVE IT A GO!

NAME	MUSCLE	MUSSEL
Gluteus maximus		
Mytilus galloprovincialis		
Modiolus modiolus		
Pectoralis major		
Perna canaliculus		
Mytilus chilensis		
Deltoid		
Gastrocnemius		
Mytilus edulis		
Rectus abdominus		

SKIN DEEP →

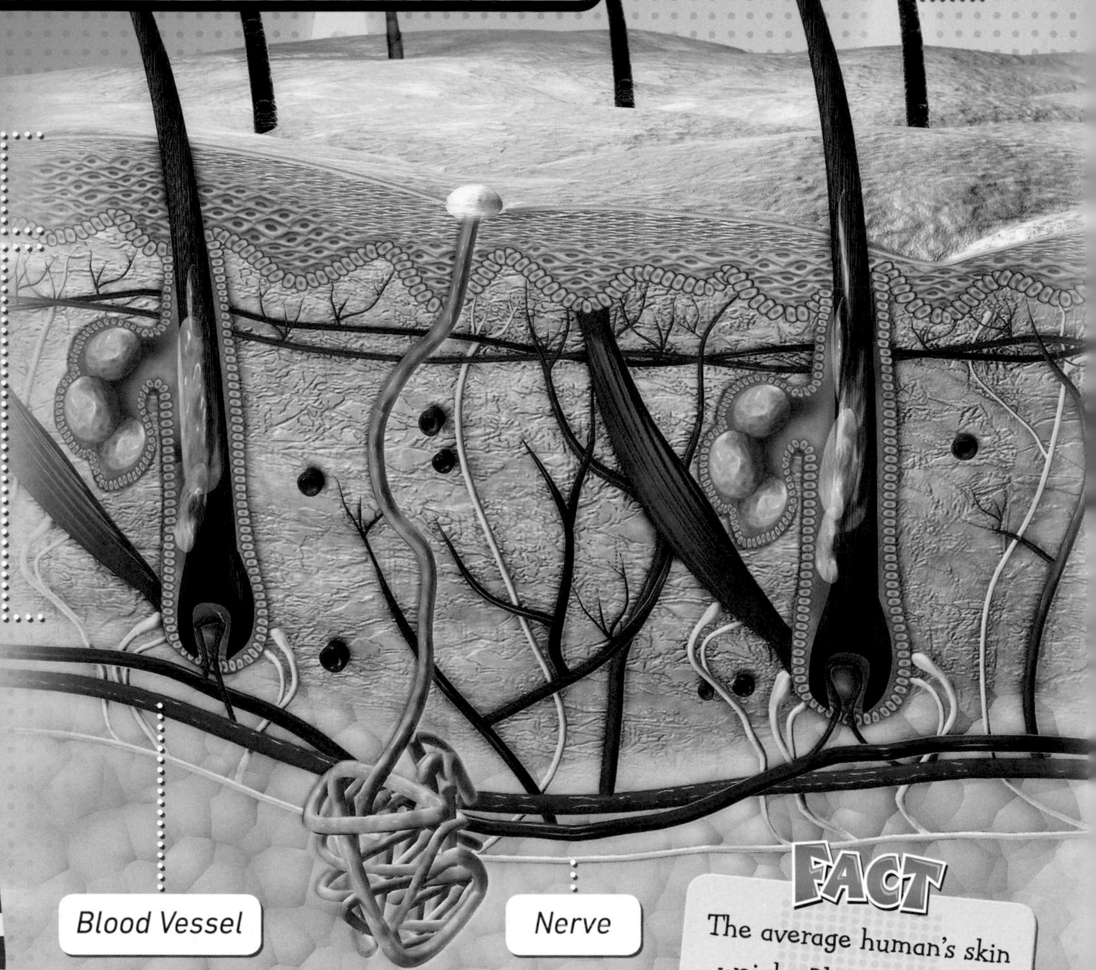

Hair

Epidermis

Dermis

DID YOU KNOW?

The outer layer of skin that you can see is called the epidermis and consists of dead cells that protect your body against things like dirt and germs! You are constantly shedding old skin cells and your body then replaces them.

Wouldn't it be cool if we lost all our skin at once like a snake?! Xand

Blood Vessel

Nerve

FACT
The average human's skin weighs 3kg – about the same as three pineapples!

Deepest Dermis

Beneath the epidermis is a thick layer called the dermis. This contains blood vessels, hair follicles, sweat glands and nerve endings.

Wrinkly Bath Skin

Ever noticed how your skin goes all wrinkly in the bath? Some scientists think it's to help you grip wet things, but Chris and Xand proved on the show that it's no help at all!

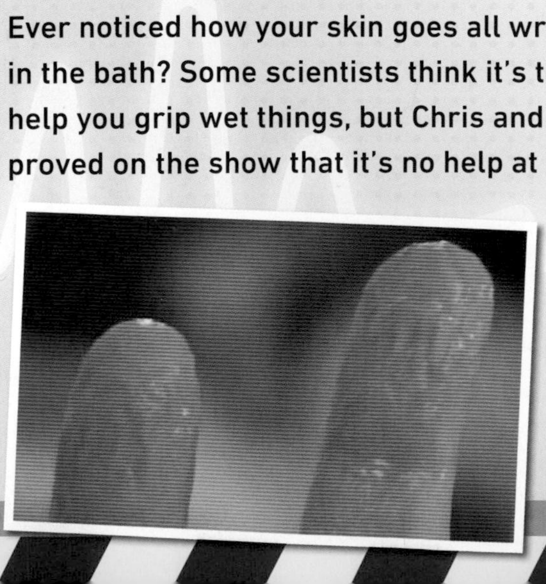

Cool Colours

Human skin comes in lots of colours, ranging from pale pink through to very dark brown. The colour of your skin depends on the amount of the pigment melanin that your body produces. Small amounts of melanin result in light skin, while large amounts result in dark skin.

FACT
Skin is our body's biggest organ.

FACT
The total skin area of a human is about 2 square metres.

OUCH! Take #97:

This is a man called Gary, who has incredibly stretchy skin. Collagen is a type of protein in the skin that keeps it flexible but strong. However, Gary has a lack of collagen, meaning he can stretch it in ways most people can't.

Skin Deep

Your skin isn't one thickness all over. In some places like your eyelids it can be as thin as 0.5mm, whereas on the soles of your feet it can be as thick as 5mm!

You'll just have to take our word for this as you can't measure the thickness of your own skin! Chris

FACT
The entire surface of your skin is replaced every month, which put another way means you have about 1,000 different skins in your life!

My personal favourite was number 261... I miss that skin... Xand

Hot & Cold

Wait, my skin doesn't have radiators on it ... Does it? Xand

YOUR SKIN PLAYS A VITAL ROLE IN YOUR BODY'S CENTRAL HEATING SYSTEM.

Just Right

Humans need to stay at around 37 degrees Celsius, and your skin has a few clever ways to help make this happen.

Guess What?

When you're hot, the blood vessels near the top of your skin widen, allowing the blood flow to your skin to increase and take heat away from your body. This is called vasodilation. When you're cold, the opposite happens. The blood vessels narrow, and the blood flow to your skin decreases. This is called vasoconstriction.

Don't Sweat It

Sweat

Actually, do sweat it! Sweating is another of your body's ways of cooling you down. Sweat glands release extra sweat on to the skin's surface when you're hot. The sweat evaporates, drawing heat from the body and cooling you down.

FACT
Sweat is 99% water.

Sweat gland

Decision Time

The body has 2.5 million sweat pores. **FACT**

Your body makes a choice about what parts of you it needs to keep warm. It prioritizes your vital organs that are necessary for life, like your heart and your brain, and allows parts that you can do without to get cold first, like your fingers and toes.

Mental note: must buy new gloves, I quite like my fingers and don't want to lose them! Chris

Clever!

To help keep you warm, the hairs on your skin stand up to help trap the heat next to your body. This was probably more effective in our ancestors who had more hair on their body. Tiny muscles make the hairs stand upright, causing little bumps on the skin that we call 'goose bumps'.

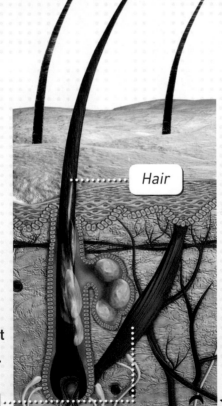
Hair

Arrector pili muscle

HONK! HONK!

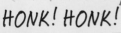
They're called goose bumps because your skin looks like the skin of a goose! Xand

DO TRY THIS AT HOME!

ALL YOU'LL NEED FOR THIS TRICK IS A FRIEND AND A PENNY . . .

1. Give the penny to your friend and then turn your back on them.

2. When you are no longer facing them, ask them to select one of their hands to hide the penny in, clench it in their fist and hold it up above their head.

3. You'll need them to keep their fist above their head for about 30 seconds, so you need to talk to them to distract them – you could tell them to focus on what hand the penny is in and say you are trying to pick up on their brainwaves.

4. When about 30 seconds have passed, tell them to put their hand down by their side, and pocket the penny.

5. Then you can turn around and ask them to put their hands out in front of them.

AND NOW FOR THE MAGIC!

6. Look closely at their hands – you'll be able to tell which hand your friend has just been holding up in the air because you won't be able to see the veins sticking up as much as the hand that was by their side. The skin on the back of our hands is relatively thin, which means you can tell the blood has drained out of the hand that was raised above their head. Give it a try at home and see if you can trick your friends!

Meet the Maggots

HANDS UP IF YOU FLICKED STRAIGHT TO THIS PAGE!

I DID!

Here are Chris' favourite pictures of the day he met the maggots!

ME TOO!

FACT
Over 50% of the dust around the home is made up of dead skin cells.

This is me in a rather silly outfit in a sterile room filled with 36,000 flies!

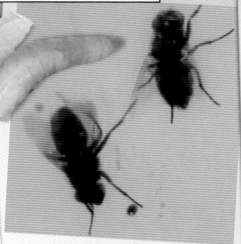
But it wasn't the flies I was interested in meeting . . .

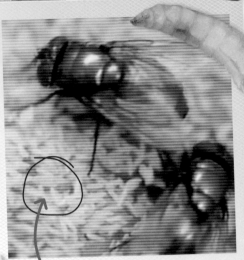
And it wasn't the eggs that they laid either . . .

It was the maggots that hatched from the eggs – yuck!

500 maggots were used to treat a nasty wound on this patient's foot!

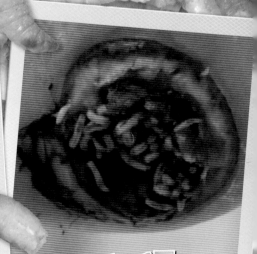

FACT
Every minute you shed over 30,000 dead skin cells.

Although they can eat dead flesh, maggots don't have any teeth. They vomit powerful chemicals on to the wound which dissolve dead flesh and the maggot can then eat that along with any bacteria that are around – and that is what makes them the perfect wound-cleaning machines!

Bruises, Scabs & Blisters

BEING THE FIRST LINE OF DEFENCE IS TOUGH ON YOUR SKIN . . .

Amazing!

Minor cuts and scratches are very common – you've probably got a cut or a scratch somewhere on your body right now. Have you noticed how they go away after time? That's because your skin heals itself by producing new cells to replace the damaged ones. A lump called a clot forms on the surface, which stops blood leaking out and stops dirt, germs and bacteria from getting in. The clot then hardens and forms a scab. Underneath the scab, your skin is busy forming a new layer. When the new layer is ready, the scab falls off and you're as good as new . . . until you get your next cut!

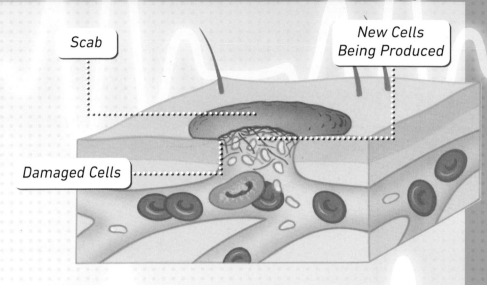

Scab

New Cells Being Produced

Damaged Cells

Brilliant Bruises

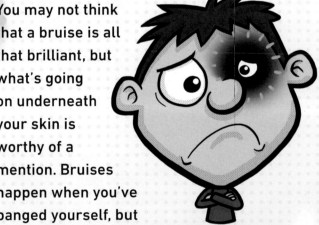

You may not think that a bruise is all that brilliant, but what's going on underneath your skin is worthy of a mention. Bruises happen when you've banged yourself, but not hard enough to break the skin. Bruises form when blood vessels under the skin get damaged and leak. The trapped blood under your skin goes through a kaleidoscope of colours as it heals – red, blue, black, purple, green and yellow! Next time you get a bruise, why not keep a bruise diary and record all the colours it goes?

Maths Time!

Maths? In a book about your body? Have we gone mad? Here's a simple maths question for you . . .

FOOT + BADLY FITTING SHOE = ?

Give yourself a round of applause if you answered 'blister'! Blisters are small cushions of fluid under the outer layers of your skin. They are basically your body's version of a plaster, protecting your skin from being damaged.

And as tempting as it can be, you should never pop your blisters. Left unpopped, your body will reabsorb the liquid when your skin is healed. Chris

Comfortable in Your Own Skin

ON THE WHOLE, THE SKIN ON YOUR BODY LOOKS THE SAME. BUT OCCASIONALLY YOU MIGHT COME ACROSS BITS THAT LOOK A LITTLE DIFFERENT . . .

DID YOU KNOW?

Freckles are caused when a group of cells of a slightly darker colour than the rest of your skin occur in small batches. They are completely harmless and tend to be found on people who have lighter skin tones. You might have some on your face, or on your shoulders, arms or legs.

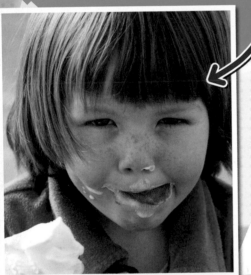

Moles

We're talking about moles that you find on your skin, of course. If you want to find out about the little creatures who live underground, you're looking in the wrong book. Skin moles form small bumps on your body (not mounds of earth in the garden!). They are often brownish in colour and look like small spots on the skin and are caused by cells called melanocytes. The medical term for moles is melanocytic naevi. Most moles are harmless – both the ones on your skin and the ones underground.

I can see why most people just use the word 'moles'! Chris

FACT
Birthmarks can appear inside your body too!

OUCH! Take #84:

Xand met a boy called James who has a birthmark shaped like Britain – check it out! Birthmarks are coloured marks that are visible on the skin, and are nothing to worry about. There are two main types of birthmark: vascular birthmarks that are often red, pink or purple and are caused by abnormal blood vessels in or under the skin; and pigmented birthmarks, which are usually brown, and are caused by clusters of pigment cells.

SPOT TO SPOT

Spots. Pimples. Zits. Whatever you call them, chances are you'll get one (or more!) on your face at some point in your life. They can occur when the oil glands in your skin get clogged up and can become swollen and red.

JOIN TOGETHER THE SPOTS BELOW TO SEE IF YOU CAN WORK OUT WHOSE FACE THIS IS . . .

If you need a clue, I can assure you that this person is very clever, and much more handsome than his brother Chris! Xand

HAIR WE GO! →

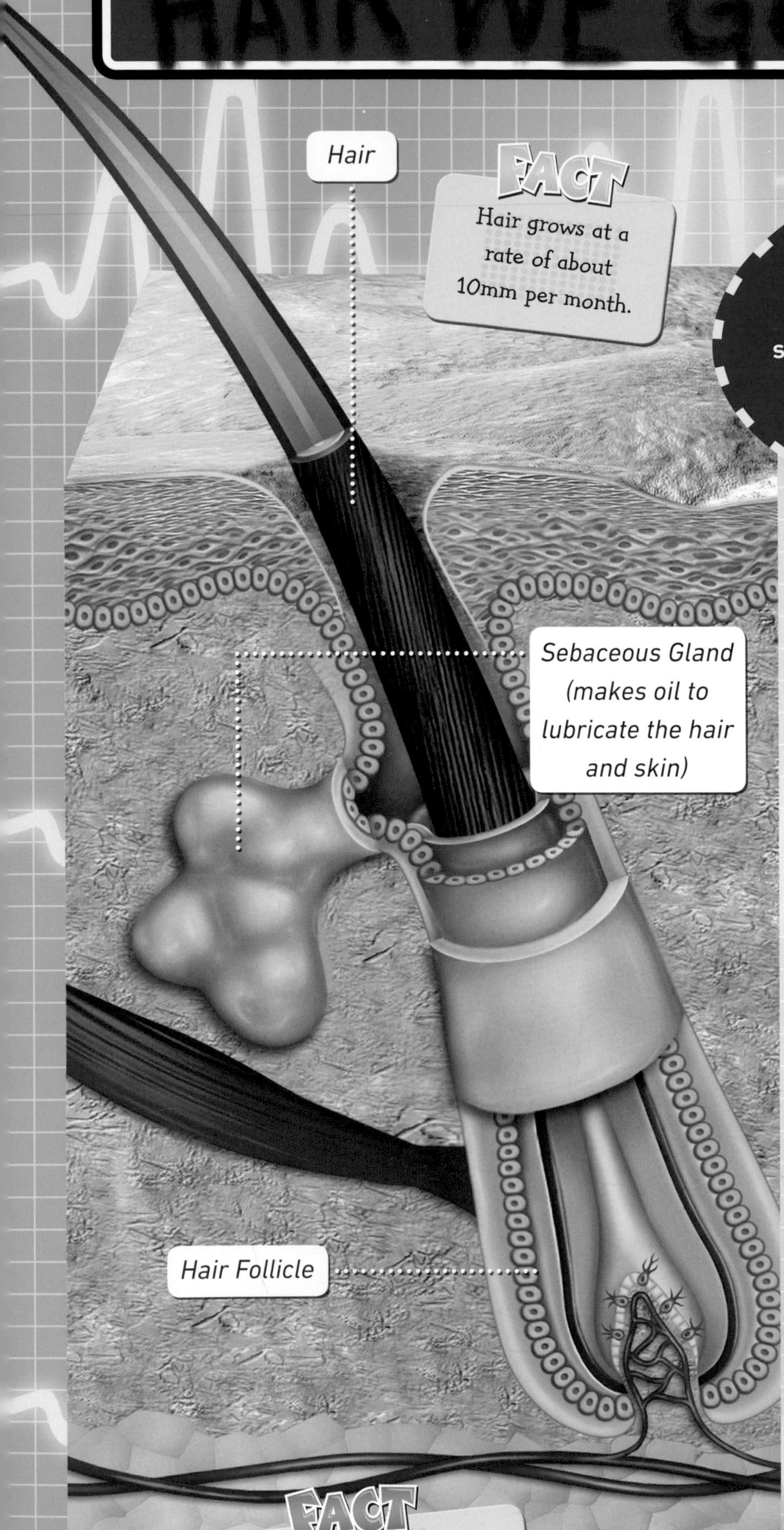

Hair

FACT
Hair grows at a rate of about 10mm per month.

DID YOU KNOW?
The number of hairs on your head ranges from around 90,000 to 140,000 depending on what sort of hair you have. People with fair hair have the most hairs, followed by those with dark hair. Those with red hair have the fewest.

I don't know about you, but I've got the hairy kind of hair! Chris

Sebaceous Gland
(makes oil to lubricate the hair and skin)

Hair Raising

The cells at the bottom of each follicle constantly divide to make new hair, pushing it to the surface. The sebaceous gland releases an oily substance called sebum to soften and lubricate the hairs.

Hair Follicle

FACT
Human hair is one of the strongest fibres on the planet.

That's Why!

Ever wondered why we have eyebrows? Well, wonder no more *Ouch!* fans. They have the very important job of stopping things like sweat and rain from getting into your eyes. They also help to communicate how you are feeling to other people, like showing whether you are confused, angry or surprised.

Check out the section on page 133 of this HuManual for more on this! Xand

RIP Hair

Did you know that the hair you can see on your head is already dead? The only living part is in the root at the base, known as a hair follicle.

Wow!

Even if you didn't cut your hair, it would usually stop growing at around 1.5m. Hair grows for two to six years, before the follicles take a rest. Around 15% of your follicles are resting at any one time!

HAIR CEMETERY

RIP

I'VE RUN OUT OF SHAMPOO, AGAIN!

FACT
Around 100 of your scalp hairs are lost and replaced each day.

The OUCH! Salon

Pick a Colour!

Hair comes in four basic colours – blond, red, brown and black. Which colour you have depends on a pigment called melanin. As most people get older, the amount of melanin decreases, meaning that the colour fades and the hair turns grey.

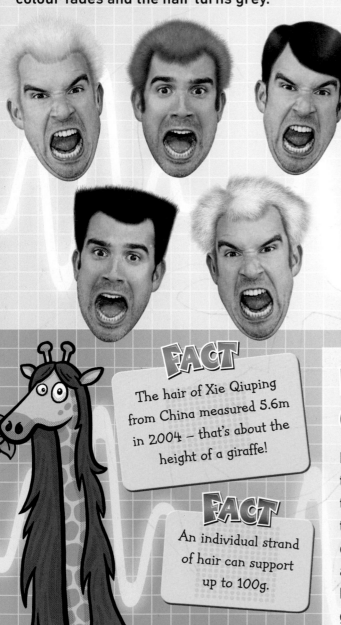

DID YOU KNOW?

Your hair can be straight, wavy or curly, but have you ever wondered why? Well, it's to do with the actual shape of your individual hairs. If you were to cut a hair in half and look at it under a microscope, you'd be able to see that each strand of straight hair is round, wavy hair is curved and curly hair is flat.

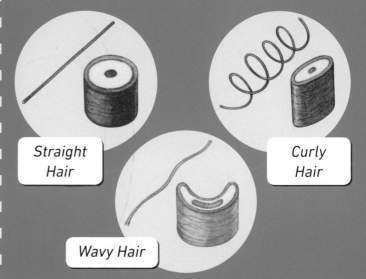

Straight Hair

Curly Hair

Wavy Hair

FACT

The hair of Xie Qiuping from China measured 5.6m in 2004 – that's about the height of a giraffe!

FACT

An individual strand of hair can support up to 100g.

Hair Today, Gone Tomorrow!

By the time they reach their thirties, 25% of men begin to lose their hair or start to go bald. This is because of changes in men's bodies as they get older. The hair becomes short and fine, and grows for just a few weeks before falling out.

FACT

At any given time, around 85% of the hair on your head is growing – the other 15% is resting!

That's a bit like Chris and me when we're filming Operation Ouch! – we spend 85% of the time working and 15% resting! Xand

Nailed It!

Nail Root

Nail Bed

Nail

FACT
On average, men's fingernails grow faster than women's.

Fingertip

Phalanx (Finger Bone)

FACT
Fingernails grow faster than toenails.

FACT
Fingernails grow an average 3.5mm per month.

Rhi-No Way!

Not only is keratin found in hair and nails, but it is also found in rhino horns!

Wow!

A man from America called Melvin Boothe had incredibly long fingernails. The combined total length of all his fingernails was 9.85m – that's a bit longer than the length of two black taxis!

Amazing!

Lee Redmond from America had rather long nails too – hers measured 8.65m in total. That's the height of two double-decker buses!

Finger Food

Do you bite your nails? If so, you might want to rethink this particular finger food. There are often germs under your fingernails, so when you bite your nails, those germs can get into your mouth. Biting your nails can also damage your teeth and gums, and the skin on your fingers. Lots of people can stop doing it easily but, if you're really struggling, it's worth asking your doctor about it.

FACT
Roughly half of 10–18 year-olds bite their nails.

WHERE DO YOU FIND GIANT SNAILS?

ON THE END OF GIANTS' FINGERS!

I DON'T KNOW

Naughty Nails

FACT

Toenails are roughly twice as thick as fingernails.

Gross!

That is gross ... but I like it!
Xand

Lots of people get something called a fungal nail infection at some point in their life, and they are more common in toenails than in fingernails. The infection can lead to the nail becoming discoloured, thickened and distorted.

Yuck!

It's caused by a kind of fungi which often live harmlessly on your skin, but occasionally they multiply and this is when infection strikes. The fungi love warm, dark and moist places, so a foot inside a sock is a perfect environment. Sometimes the infection goes away on its own, but if it's a bad case, you may need to get medical help.

When we were filming Ouch And About, I met someone called Cassius who had a fungal infection. I suggested a couple of tips: you can get medical help, like an anti-fungal treatment that you paint on the nail, or you can wear quite loose-fitting shoes that breathe easily, and on sunny days you could just wear flip-flops! — *Chris*

Toe-tally Painful!

An ingrown toenail is when the sides of the toenail actually start to grow into the surrounding skin. It can be very painful when the nail pierces the skin and your toe starts to look red, swollen and tender. But don't worry if you ever have an ingrown toenail because there are lots of treatments that your doctor can suggest that can help.

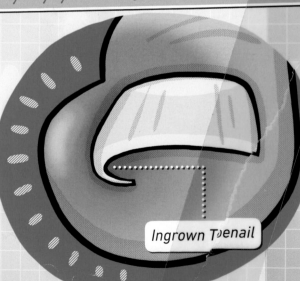

Ingrown Toenail

FACT

Nails grow faster in the summer than in the winter.

FACT

The fastest-growing nail is the one on your middle finger, the slowest is your thumbnail.

Nail Art

IT'S TIME TO GET CREATIVE!

Lots of people like to use nail polish to paint their nails different colours. Some people even stick gems on their nails to give them a bit of sparkle.

So, grab your pens, pencils, crayons, paints or glitter — whatever you can find — and decorate the nails on this page with your own nail designs. You could go for a solid colour, or maybe spots and stripes, or even the *Operation Ouch!* logo!

Phalanges

Terrific Tools

Your hands are pretty handy when you think about it. With a complex structure of bones covered with muscles, tendons and skin, they are amazing tools that you use all the time. They help you do all sorts of things, from picking up objects to much more intricate actions like using a pen to write your name.

Don't forget about picking your nose too! Xand

Enough already, Xand! Chris

Metacarpals

Wow!

Each hand contains 27 bones, so if you add both hands together, they make up for over a quarter of the bones in your whole body. The bones in your fingers and thumbs are called phalanges and each hand has 14 of them. The bones in the palm of your hand are called your metacarpals. The combination of these bones with the joints between them is what gives your hands their flexibility.

FACT
Around 90% of people are right-handed and just 10% are left-handed. Truly ambidextrous people (who are equally comfortable with either hand) are very rare.

Carpals

Thumbs Up for Thumbs!

Unlike most animals, we have opposable thumbs. You probably take it for granted that your thumb can touch each of your fingers on the same hand, but only humans and primates like apes can do this. This allows us to handle objects and use things like paintbrushes and pencils.

Great for messaging your mates! Chris

Carping Around

There are eight carpal bones: scaphoid, lunate, triquetrum, pisiform, trapezium, trapezoid, capitate and hamate. Here's a handy way of remembering them: Sam Likes To Push The Toy Car Home. Memorize that and it'll give you a nice head start in medical school!

FACT

You have more than 250,000 sweat glands on each foot – that's more than anywhere else on your body!

Amazing!

The human foot is an amazing 'feat' of engineering! It's built just like an arched bridge, combining mechanical complexity with structural strength. Your ankle does lots of jobs including: supporting your body, reducing impact from activities like walking, running and jumping, and of course helping you to move.

Tarsals

Metatarsals

Phalanges

WHAT KIND OF TREE GROWS ON YOUR HAND?

I DON'T KNOW

A PALM TREE!

IF YOU HAD FIVE APPLES IN ONE HAND, AND FIVE ORANGES IN THE OTHER, WHAT WOULD YOU HAVE?

I DON'T KNOW

MASSIVE HANDS!

DID YOU KNOW?

Your feet contain 52 bones between them, so your hands and feet combined contain half the bones in your whole body! Just like your hands, your feet have phalanges, but rather than metacarpals, your feet have bones called metatarsals.

Wicked Warts & Vicious Verrucas

Wart Are They?

Common warts have a raised cauliflower-like appearance and are skin coloured. They are hard and rough and usually occur on fingers, the backs of hands and sometimes knees.

Verruca-verse

Verrucas are more flattened, with hard outer edges, and often have small black spots in the centre. They are normally found on the ball of the foot, the bottoms of toes, or on the heel.

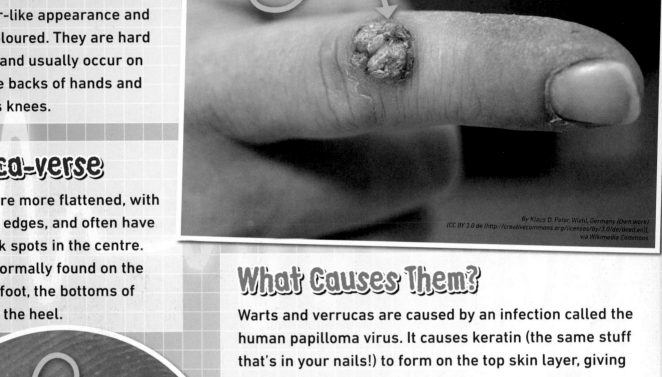

By Klaus D. Peter, Wiehl, Germany (Own work)
(CC BY 3.0 de (http://creativecommons.org/licenses/by/3.0/de/deed.en)),
via Wikimedia Commons

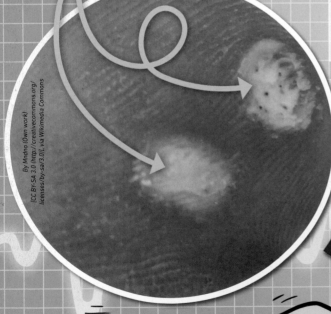

By Mndno (Own work)
(CC BY-SA 3.0 (http://creativecommons.org/
licenses/by-sa/3.0)), via Wikimedia Commons

What Causes Them?

Warts and verrucas are caused by an infection called the human papilloma virus. It causes keratin (the same stuff that's in your nails!) to form on the top skin layer, giving the rough, hard texture of a wart.

Wart Next?

Most warts and verrucas will go away on their own, but this can take a long time. Your doctor will be able to tell you about lots of treatments that are available if it bothers you or causes any pain.

Don't touch!

Warts and verrucas are very contagious, so as tempting as it might be to poke and prod them, try not to touch them!

Xand's Verruca

EVEN DOCTORS HAVE TO GET TREATMENT FOR THINGS LIKE VERRUCAS. HERE'S WHAT HAPPENED WHEN XAND VISITED THE PODIATRIST (THAT'S A FANCY NAME FOR A FOOT DOCTOR!).

Meet my feet! They look OK in a sort of foolish way, don't they? But look a little closer . . .

Meet my verrucas!

To begin the treatment, the podiatrist scraped off the hard skin using a scalpel — it didn't hurt and actually tickled a bit!

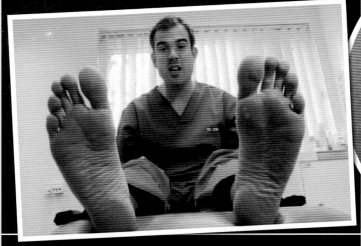

Next, liquid nitrogen was applied to freeze the verruca. Liquid nitrogen is incredibly cold (−200ºC(!), so there was a bit of pain, even for a tough doctor like me!

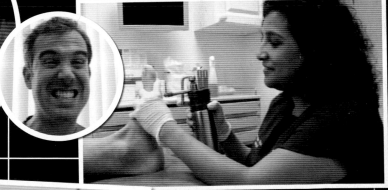

Finally, a layer of silver nitrate was applied. This is a special substance that stops blistering and helps kill the virus.

I gave my verruca a name — **Dr Chris!** Just don't tell him!

Xand

DO TRY THIS AT HOME!

HERE'S A TRICK THAT YOU CAN PLAY ON YOUR OWN HANDS!

1. First up, you'll need to get three bowls.

2. You need to fill the first bowl with ice-cold water. The next should have water that is at room temperature. And finally, the third bowl should contain hot water (but not hot enough to scald you, so definitely not from the kettle!).

3. Now, put one hand in the bowl of ice-cold water and the other hand in the bowl of hot water and leave them there for a minute.

4. After a minute, immediately put both hands into the bowl that contains room-temperature water.

What do you notice?

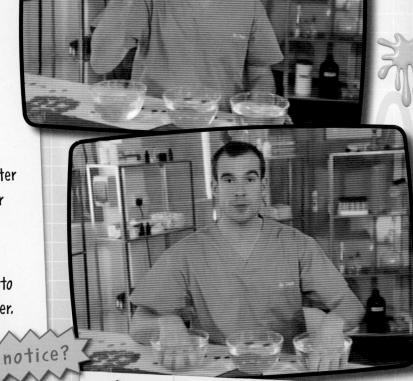

5. Even though you know that the water is the same temperature, the hand that was in the ice-cold water will now feel hot and the hand that was in the hot water will now feel cold. You've successfully managed to mess with your own mind!

WHY NOT TRY IT OUT ON YOUR FRIENDS AND CONFUSE THEIR BRAINS TOO?

FINGER FUN!

HERE'S SOME FINGER FUN THAT YOU CAN TRY YOURSELF!

MIDDLE FINGER

INDEX FINGER

RING FINGER

LITTLE FINGER

Place your thumb and fingertips on the thumb and fingerprint guides on this page. You'll notice that there isn't a fingerprint to place your middle finger on, so tuck that under your palm.

THUMB

1. Now, lift up your thumb. Easy, right?

2. Next, lift up your index finger. Simple!

3. Try lifting your little finger. Again, not difficult.

4. Finally, try lifting your ring finger.

WHOA! IT'S IMPOSSIBLE, ISN'T IT?

WHY DON'T YOU GET YOUR FRIENDS AND FAMILY TO HAVE A GO!

The science bit!

This works, or rather your ring finger DOESN'T work, because all your fingers have separate muscles except for your middle finger and ring finger. The muscle that controls these fingers is connected, so you can move your ring finger when your middle finger is out, but not when it's tucked away!

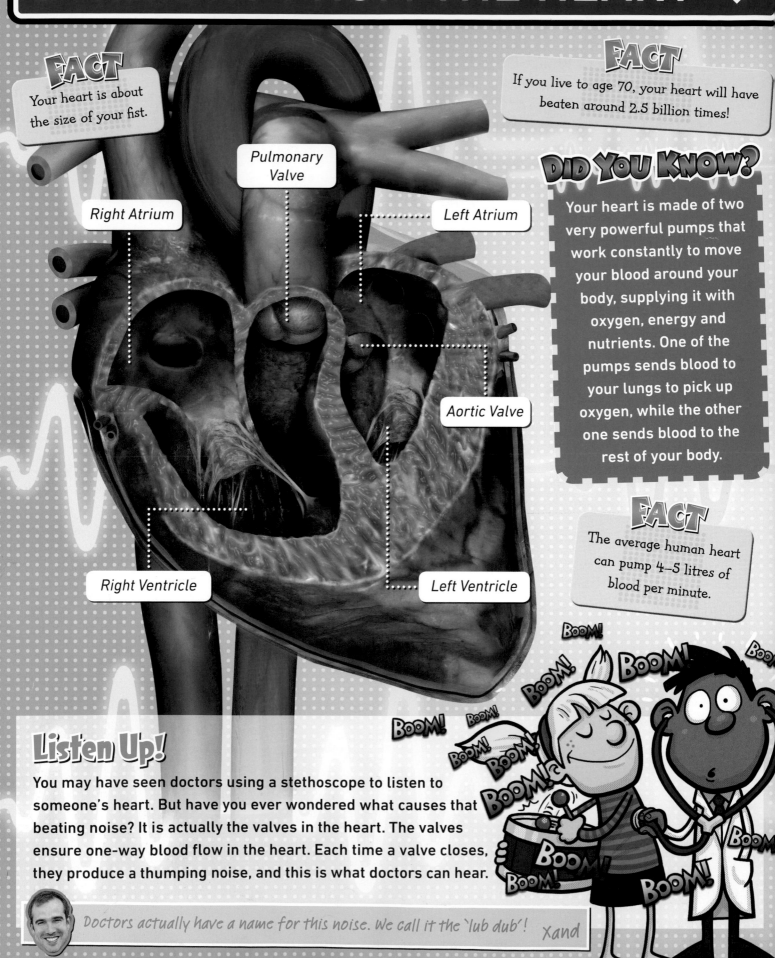

FACT
Your heart is about the size of your fist.

FACT
Your heart is about the size of your fist.

FACT
If you live to age 70, your heart will have beaten around 2.5 billion times!

Pulmonary Valve

Right Atrium

Left Atrium

DID YOU KNOW?
Your heart is made of two very powerful pumps that work constantly to move your blood around your body, supplying it with oxygen, energy and nutrients. One of the pumps sends blood to your lungs to pick up oxygen, while the other one sends blood to the rest of your body.

Aortic Valve

FACT
The average human heart can pump 4–5 litres of blood per minute.

Right Ventricle

Left Ventricle

Listen Up!

You may have seen doctors using a stethoscope to listen to someone's heart. But have you ever wondered what causes that beating noise? It is actually the valves in the heart. The valves ensure one-way blood flow in the heart. Each time a valve closes, they produce a thumping noise, and this is what doctors can hear.

BOOM! BOOM! BOOM! BOOM! BOOM! BOOM! BOOM! BOOM! BOOM! BOOM! BOOM!

Doctors actually have a name for this noise. We call it the 'lub dub'!   Xand

Beat This!

Your heart is a muscle and, as it contracts, it sends blood around the body. When it relaxes, more blood flows into the heart. Blood is carried away from your heart by blood vessels called arteries, and it's brought back by blood vessels called veins.

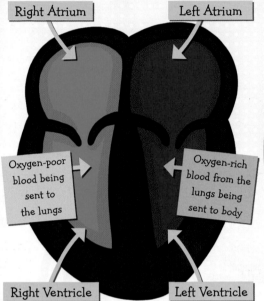

Right Atrium

Left Atrium

Oxygen-poor blood being sent to the lungs

Oxygen-rich blood from the lungs being sent to body

Right Ventricle

Left Ventricle

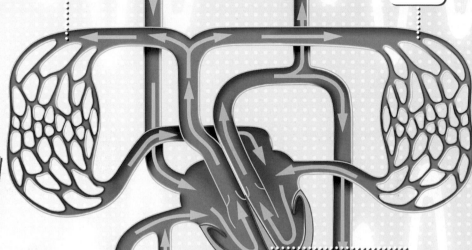

Upper Body

Lungs

Heart

Lower Body

A Chamber of Secrets

Ever wonder what goes on inside your heart? Well, the heart is divided into two halves, the left side and the right side. Each half has two chambers, a smaller one called the upper atrium and a larger, thicker ventricle. It is the right part of the heart that receives blood from the body before sending it to the lungs to pick up oxygen. The left side receives this oxygen-rich blood from the lungs, before sending it out to the body.

On the Pulse

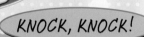

As blood surges through your arteries, it makes them bulge slightly. This creates something called your pulse. Medical staff sometimes check your pulse to find out how quickly blood is flowing around your body.

KNOCK, KNOCK!

WHO'S THERE?

HEART

HEART WHO?

HEART TO HEAR YOU, PLEASE SPEAK UP!

DO TRY THIS AT HOME!

Wow!

Lots of the functions of the body happen under the skin and it can be a bit difficult to work out exactly what is happening. However, your heart rate is something that you can monitor yourself, and there's no surgery required!

FACT

Before the invention of the stethoscope, doctors had to press their ear to a patient's chest.

CHECK IT OUT!

You can check the pulse in your wrist by holding your palm upwards and putting your index finger and your middle finger on the inside of your wrist on the thumb side of your hand. Then press lightly until you feel a throb — this is your pulse.

READY, SET, GO!

Have a stopwatch or a clock nearby and count how many times you can feel your pulse in 60 seconds. This will tell you what your resting heart rate is. Depending on your age, your heart rate should be somewhere between 60 and 100 beats per minute.

MOVE IT!

If you do some exercise and then check your pulse, you'll find that your heart rate has gone up. This is because your muscles need more oxygen when you exercise, so your heart has to get blood around your body more quickly.

HEART TO HEART

Just like doctors and nurses measure other people's heart rate, so can you! Why don't you offer to take the pulse of your friends or family and see how their heart rate compares to yours.

FACT

The symbol of a heart is used to show love because people used to think that our heart controlled emotion. We now know that it is the brain that is responsible. A picture of a brain on a Valentine's Day card wouldn't be quite the same, would it?

My Valentine

Heart Help

Body Battle

Do you know what a heart attack is? The word 'attack' sounds like there's a fight or a battle going on, and that's kind of what is happening within the heart of someone who's having a heart attack. It is a battle between the body and an attack on their heart.

What Is It?

A heart attack happens when there is a blockage in the heart that stops the blood from moving around freely. This can be dangerous because your body relies on fresh blood and all the things it contains like oxygen, energy and nutrients, to function.

FACT

A woman's average heart rate is faster than a man's by almost eight beats per minute.

FACT

The study of the human heart is known as cardiology.

The Signs

There are lots of signs to look for in someone who could be having a heart attack. These include chest pains, pains in other areas of the body, feeling dizzy, and sweating, amongst others. It is important that an ambulance is called for anyone who might be having a heart attack so that they can get treatment as soon as possible.

Emergency Response

Heart attacks are one of the most common reasons why a person requires emergency medical treatment. Paramedic Jan Vann, who Chris and Xand often join when they go On Call, attends lots of emergencies where people are suffering from heart attacks.

PARAMEDIC JAN VANN

The British Heart Foundation estimates that around 50,000 men and 32,000 women have a heart attack each year in England alone, with most heart attacks occurring in people aged over 45.

FACT

Heart disease has been detected in 3,000 year-old Egyptian mummies.

Brilliant Blood

Amazing

When you first think of blood, you might not realize how brilliant it actually is. After all, most people only ever get to see their own blood when they have hurt themselves . . . and that's never a good thing!

3 in 1!

Your blood contains three types of cell, all with their own role to play. Red blood cells give blood its colour and take oxygen from the lungs and carry it around the body. White blood cells fight disease and help remove waste from the body. And finally there are cells called platelets that help the blood clot. Clots are like plugs that stop blood leaking.

FACT
Adults have around five litres of blood in their bodies.

FACT
The most common blood type in the UK is O+, followed by A+, B+ and O−.

FACT
Hospitals in the UK use around 4,000 litres of blood every day.

Blood Vessel

Red Blood Cell

Platelets

White Blood Cell

DID YOU KNOW?

Blood comes in different types. There are four blood groups: A, B, AB and O. These groups are divided further into positive and negative. If you need to be given blood in hospital, the medical team will need to know what blood type you are so they can give you the right sort.

WHAT WOULD YOU GET IF YOU CROSSED A VAMPIRE WITH A TEACHER?

I DON'T KNOW

LOTS OF BLOOD TESTS!

Hospitals need blood all the time to help them treat sick people, so donating blood is a really good thing to do!

Chris

Round and Round and Round

YOUR BLOOD VESSELS ARE LIKE A ROAD SYSTEM IN YOUR BODY, WITH YOUR BLOOD CELLS SPEEDING ROUND AND ROUND AND ROUND . . . THIS NETWORK OF VESSELS IS CALLED YOUR CIRCULATORY SYSTEM. GET READY TO GO ON A JOURNEY!

Road Map of You

Your heart is like a bus station where all the blood cells depart and then make drop-offs and pick-ups around the body. The blood cells travel along major arteries and veins, which are like motorways and main roads, and then they travel along small capillaries, which are like much narrower country lanes. Take a look at this 'map' inside you . . .

FACT

Blood cells travel super-quickly from your heart to the furthest reaches of your body, and then back to your heart again. The journey from your heart to the tip of your big toe and back again can take as little as 20 seconds, and on average only takes about a minute.

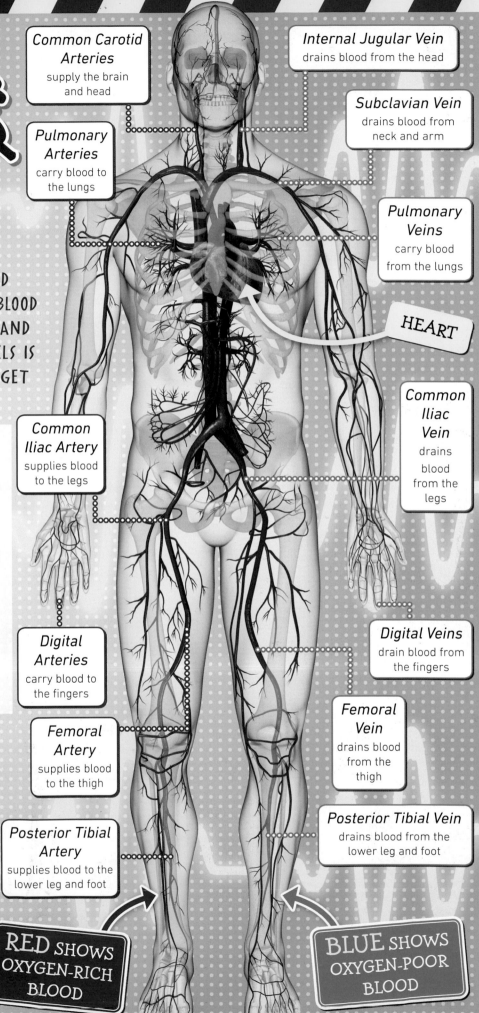

Common Carotid Arteries supply the brain and head

Pulmonary Arteries carry blood to the lungs

Internal Jugular Vein drains blood from the head

Subclavian Vein drains blood from neck and arm

Pulmonary Veins carry blood from the lungs

HEART

Common Iliac Artery supplies blood to the legs

Common Iliac Vein drains blood from the legs

Digital Arteries carry blood to the fingers

Digital Veins drain blood from the fingers

Femoral Artery supplies blood to the thigh

Femoral Vein drains blood from the thigh

Posterior Tibial Artery supplies blood to the lower leg and foot

Posterior Tibial Vein drains blood from the lower leg and foot

RED SHOWS OXYGEN-RICH BLOOD

BLUE SHOWS OXYGEN-POOR BLOOD

Lovely Leeches

Gross!

Leeches are blood-sucking worms that are capable of consuming five times their own body weight in blood in one sitting.

That would be the same as me eating an entire baby cow – hooves, horns and all, in just one meal! Greedy! Chris

BEFORE

AFTER

FACT
Some leeches can have 125 teeth.

FACT
Each leech is both male and female.

Medical Marvels

Surgeons are able to use leeches in amazing ways. For example, imagine you've accidentally cut off half your finger – ouch! A surgeon could join the finger back together. However, if blood clots have formed inside the end that fell off, new blood from the rest of your body wouldn't be able to get to it and the end of your finger would eventually die and fall off. By attaching a leech to the tip of the finger, the chemicals in its saliva allow blood to flow by dissolving any clots, and supplying the reattached finger with fresh blood.

Life Savers

Leeches can save lives! They do this by making a small bite in your skin and releasing saliva, or spit, into your veins. A chemical in their saliva thins your blood, which prevents it from clotting, meaning that a scab doesn't form and blood flows freely into their bellies. Leeches are only used in medicine by experts, so don't try using them yourself!

FACT
Leeches have 32 brains!

That's 31.5 more than my brother appears to have most of the time! Chris

WHY DID THE LEECH WANT TO BE AN ARTIST?

I DON'T KNOW, XAND, WHY DID THE LEECH WANT TO BE AN ARTIST?

BECAUSE SHE WAS GOOD AT DRAWING BLOOD!

Leech Farms

The ability of leeches to help in surgery is more effective than any machine that has been invented, which means that there are farms that breed them for medical use. Leeches lay their eggs in nests that start out as balls of foam and end up looking a bit like sponges.

The Blood Test

NORMAL BLOOD TESTS INVOLVE NEEDLES . . . BUT NOT THIS ONE! SEE HOW YOU GET ON!

1. The heart is divided into two parts, but what do we call these?

A. *the left side and right side*

B. *the upper side and the lower side*

2. What is your heart about the size of?

A. *a walnut*

B. *a fist*

C. *a football*

3. The circulatory system is made of arteries, capillaries and what else?

A. *veins*

B. *planes*

C. *trains*

4. Roughly how many litres of blood does an adult have in their body?

A. *5 litres*

B. *15 litres*

C. *50 litres*

5. How many teeth do some leeches have?

A. *12*   **B.** *25*   **C.** *125*

6. How many times does a human heart beat in an average lifetime?

A. *2.5 million*

B. *2.5 billion*

C. *2.5 trillion*

7. What do doctors use to listen to your heart?

A. *a horoscope*

B. *a telescope*

C. *a stethoscope*

8. How many times round the world would the blood vessels in your body reach?

A. *1.5 times*

B. *2.5 times*

C. *10 times*

9. **True** or **false**: the blood in your veins is actually blue.

10. How long does it take for the heart to pump blood around your body?

A. *one minute*

B. *one hour*

C. *one day*

FIND OUT HOW YOU DID ON PAGE 173!

YOUR LIVELY LIVER →

Phew!

If there were medals for hard-working parts of your body, your liver would definitely be in the running! Located in the very middle of your abdomen, it carries out more than 500 different functions including removing poison from your blood, storing sugar, fats, copper, iron and vitamins, plus it makes digestive juices, regulates cholesterol, and removes old red blood cells.

TOP OF THE CLASS

DID YOU KNOW?

What does your liver have in common with Doctor Who? They can both regenerate! Even if you lost three quarters of your liver, it would be able to regrow to full size again.

Central Heating

With its location in the centre of your body, and all the work it does, your liver is almost like an inbuilt central heating system that helps control your body temperature.

Actually it's even better than central heating, because your lovely liver does it for free!

Xand

FACT
At any given time, 10% of your body's blood is in your liver.

LIVER

Stomach

Large Intestine

Small Intestine

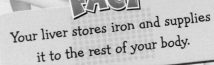

FACT
Your liver stores iron and supplies it to the rest of your body.

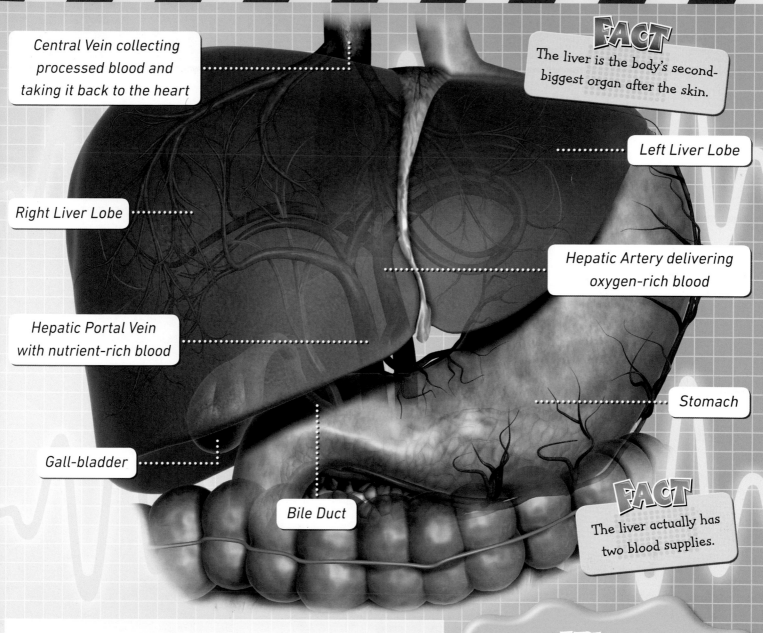

Central Vein collecting processed blood and taking it back to the heart

FACT
The liver is the body's second-biggest organ after the skin.

Left Liver Lobe

Right Liver Lobe

Hepatic Artery delivering oxygen-rich blood

Hepatic Portal Vein with nutrient-rich blood

Stomach

Gall-bladder

Bile Duct

FACT
The liver actually has two blood supplies.

Processing Plant

The main work that the liver does takes place inside your lobules. It's a good word and they're good things! Lobules are powerful processing plants but they are tiny – each one is about the size of a sesame seed that you might find on a burger bun!

A LOBULE IS THE SIZE OF A SESAME SEED

Vile Bile!

The liver produces something called bile. Bile is mainly made of water, but also contains a type of salt that helps digest fats. Bile also helps to break down waste matter from red blood cells, and this is what makes your poo brown.

EVERY BREATH YOU TAKE →

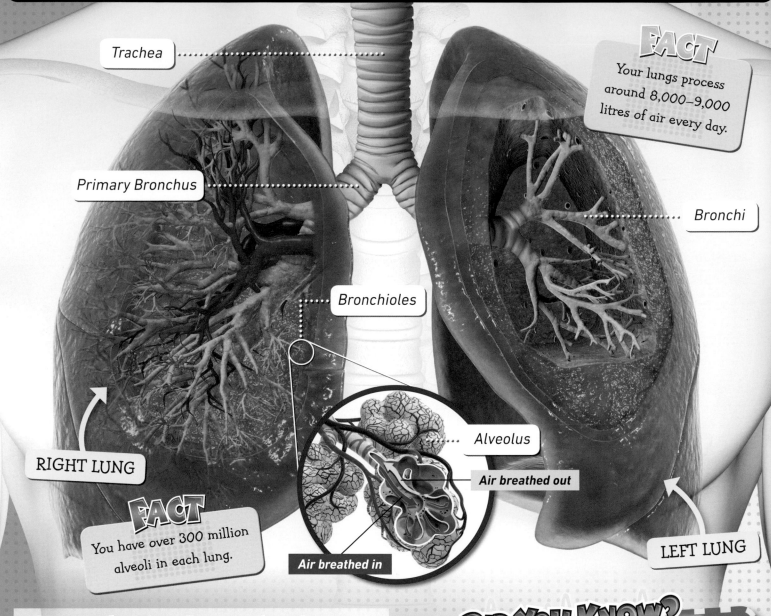

Trachea

Primary Bronchus

Bronchioles

Bronchi

Alveolus

Air breathed out

Air breathed in

RIGHT LUNG

LEFT LUNG

FACT
Your lungs process around 8,000–9,000 litres of air every day.

FACT
You have over 300 million alveoli in each lung.

Breathe In, Breathe Out

Right now, you're breathing. Breathing is something that your body does automatically without you even having to think about it. Which is really lucky because you breathe about 20,000 times a day and having to actively think about doing this would get very annoying!

IN

OUT

DID YOU KNOW?

Every cell in your body needs oxygen to function. You breathe in air that contains oxygen (among other things), your blood carries this oxygen around your body and then you breathe out carbon dioxide. Your body is unable to survive more than a few minutes without oxygen.

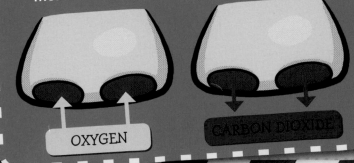

OXYGEN

CARBON DIOXIDE

Where?

The air you breathe in goes directly into your lungs where it is processed. You have two lungs and, in case you didn't know, they're in your chest! The inside looks a bit like upside-down trees. A thick 'trunk', called your trachea or windpipe, takes air from your mouth and nose. The trachea then splits into two main 'branches', called bronchi. Then these split into 'twigs', called bronchioles. Finally at the end are tiny air sacs called alveoli.

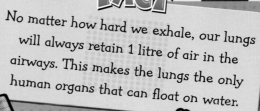

FACT

No matter how hard we exhale, our lungs will always retain 1 litre of air in the airways. This makes the lungs the only human organs that can float on water.

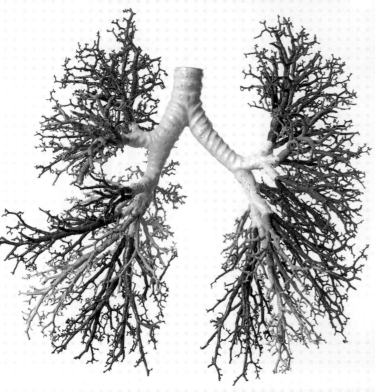

Wow!

Your lungs don't actually make themselves shrink and expand with each breath. This is controlled through your diaphragm and your ribcage. When you inhale, the diaphragm, which is a domed sheet of muscle under your lungs, contracts and pulls downwards whilst your ribcage is pulled upwards and outwards by your intercostal muscles. As you exhale, the diaphragm relaxes and is pushed upwards and your ribcage sinks downwards and inwards.

FACT

Adult lungs have a combined weight of about 1.3kg.

Asthma Answers

What is Asthma?

Asthma is a very common lung condition that affects an estimated one million kids in the UK. You might even have it yourself. Every time you breathe, air travels down your windpipe and into your bronchi in your lungs. However, in people with asthma, the bronchi can swell and become narrow, which causes wheezing and can lead to something called an asthma attack.

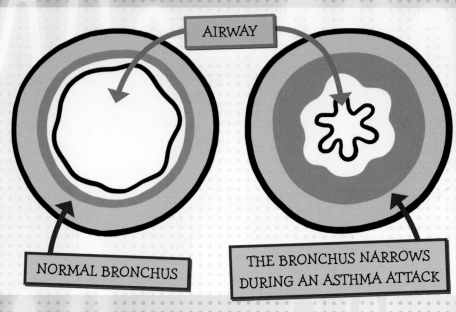

AIRWAY

NORMAL BRONCHUS

THE BRONCHUS NARROWS DURING AN ASTHMA ATTACK

What Is an Inhaler?

People with asthma are often given things called inhalers to help them live a normal life. There are different-coloured ones that have different jobs to do. Some will reduce swelling in the airways to help prevent an attack and others will calm swelling and allow air through, even if someone is having an attack.

Asthma Inhaler

How Do You Test for Asthma?

Doctors have lots of ways to test whether you have asthma, and if you do how bad it is. They can also work out the best type of treatment. One of the machines that they use is called a spirometer. It works by measuring how big a breath you take in and how quickly you can blow that air out, showing whether there is any narrowing of the airways.

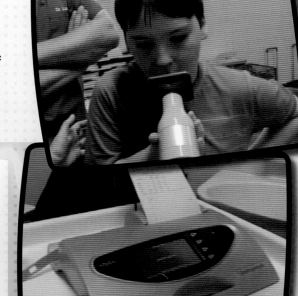

Does It Last Forever?

Asthma is actually the most common long-term health problem in the UK. Some people grow out of asthma, while others have it for life. However, it can actually be really well managed with regular check-ups and the right medication, which means that it doesn't have to impact on your life.

CITY OR SEASIDE?

Snot More Mucus!

When you breathe in air, your lungs transfer the oxygen to your blood to keep your body going. But your lungs also have to work hard to keep pollution out. And to do that they need mucus and snot.

If not, go back to pages 38 and 39 to find out! Xand

DID YOU KNOW?

All *Ouch!* fans know that you have snot up your nose. The liquidy mucus that makes snot also goes all the way down your airways to your lungs, where it traps pollution particles. This is where mucus is brilliant — it actually helps your body get rid of those particles. Tiny hairs in your lungs called cilia move the particles out of your lungs so that you can cough or spit them out!

Magnified Mucus

Here are two samples of snot that have been magnified using a microscope. One was taken from someone in a city and the other from someone at the seaside. Can you work out which is which from the amount of pollution particles trapped in the mucus?

1.

2.

BONUS CLUE!

REMEMBER, THE AIR IN THE CITY IS NORMALLY MORE POLLUTED THAN THAT AT THE SEASIDE.

CALL THE Dog-tor!

CHRIS AND XAND WERE JOINED IN THE LAB BY A VERY SPECIAL FOUR-LEGGED COLLEAGUE . . .

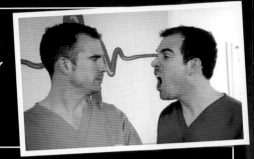

Everyone gets bad breath from time to time, and it's usually because of something we've eaten. However, your breath can also contain information about you and your health. For example, people with asthma tend to have more nitric oxide in their breath, whereas people with diabetes may have increased levels of acetone.

However, lots of medical conditions can't be detected by doctors or even clever equipment, but they can be smelt by dogs.

MEET DAISY!

Daisy can detect serious illnesses like cancer, just by smelling people's breath. To test this out, Daisy's trainer Claire brought in a sponge that had been breathed on by someone who was unwell.

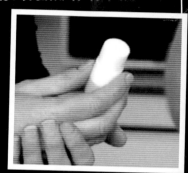

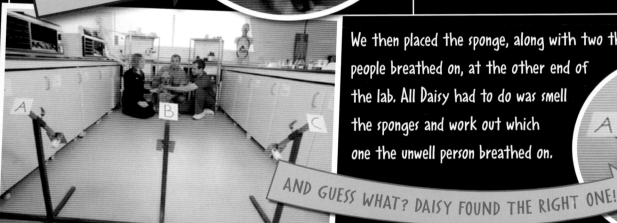

We then placed the sponge, along with two that healthy people breathed on, at the other end of the lab. All Daisy had to do was smell the sponges and work out which one the unwell person breathed on.

AND GUESS WHAT? DAISY FOUND THE RIGHT ONE!

Daisy has been trained to do this, but she doesn't actually have any more smell receptors than any other dog. Just like Daisy, Sooty and Spike each have 220,000,000 receptors. Humans only have about 5,000,000.

SOOTY

SPIKE

GIVE THAT DOG-TOR A BONE!

Lung Fun

THE LUNG AND SHORT OF IT IS THAT BY NOW YOU SHOULD BE READY FOR THIS LITTLE TEST – SO TAKE A DEEP BREATH AND SEE HOW YOU GET ON!

1. What carries air from your mouth to your lungs?

A. *drainpipe*   **B.** *hosepipe*   **C.** *windpipe*

2. How many times do you breathe each day?

A. *2,000*   **B.** *20,000*   **C.** *200,000*

3. What helps your lungs filter out particles in the air?

A. *snot*   **B.** *superbugs*   **C.** *a nose net*

4. Roughly how many alveoli do you have in each lung?

A. *3 million*   **B.** *30 million*   **C.** *300 million*

5. **True** or **false**: one lung is bigger than the other.

6. Some medical conditions can be smelt by . . .

A. *ducks*   **B.** *dogs*   **C.** *donkeys*

7. What is another name for your windpipe?

A. *tractor*   **B.** *traction*   **C.** *trachea*

8. Which of these is a machine that is used for testing asthma?

A. *spirometer*   **B.** *spinomater*   **C.** *spitometer*

9. How many litres of air do your lungs process in an average day?

A. *about 8-9*   **B.** *about 800-900*   **C.** *about 8,000–9,000*

10. The lungs are the only human organs that . . .

A. *are bigger than the liver*   **B.** *can float on water*   **C.** *never grow*

10/10

HOW MANY DID YOU GET RIGHT? FIND OUT ON PAGE 173!

DESTINATION DIGESTION →

WHEN YOU PUT FOOD INTO YOUR **MOUTH/MUSH/CAKEHOLE**, THIS IS THE BEGINNING OF A DAY-LONG JOURNEY IN WHICH THE FOOD PASSES THROUGH YOUR **STOMACH/TUMMY/BELLY** AND ENDS AT YOUR **BOTTOM/BUM/BOTTY.**

Why are there so many words for different parts of your body? It makes my HEAD/NOGGIN/BONCE hurt! Xand

The Tract Train

Food is chewed in your mouth, then it travels down your oesophagus into your stomach, next through the small and large intestines, and finally passing through your rectum and anus, with the final destination being your toilet. This whole process is called your digestive tract.

IT'S TIME TO GET ON BOARD THE TRACT TRAIN!

Mouth
All aboard! Food enters here and is the last time it sees daylight until the end of the journey. Food is mixed with saliva to make an easily swallowable mushy pulp.

Oesophagus
The food moves down a long tunnel structure called your oesophagus as it journeys towards your stomach.

Tongue
Just like train station staff, your tongue helps to make sure everything heads in the right direction, and in this case your tongue manoeuvres the food to your upper throat as you swallow. The epiglottis closes the entrance to your windpipe to make sure that the food doesn't end up in your lungs.

Stomach
Chemicals in your stomach start to break down your food as soon as it arrives. Depending on what you've eaten, food can stay here for between one and four hours, although fatty foods can take longer. The entrance and exit of the stomach have rings of muscle called sphincters — they stop anything solid escaping the stomach station until it is ready to leave.

Small Intestine
Your food arrives from the stomach into the small intestine as a thick, dark, mushy substance. The small intestine is a long, windy, coiled tube in your lower abdomen. Whilst the food is in here, the process of breaking it down and absorbing its nutrients continues.

9 Metres

Large Intestine
The last remaining nutrients and water are removed from what's left of your food in the large intestine.

Rectum & Anus
When the large intestine is finished, the food matter is squished into a short tube called your rectum. And then after this, it is squeezed out as poo from the double ring of muscles called your anus. Daylight once again!

EXIT

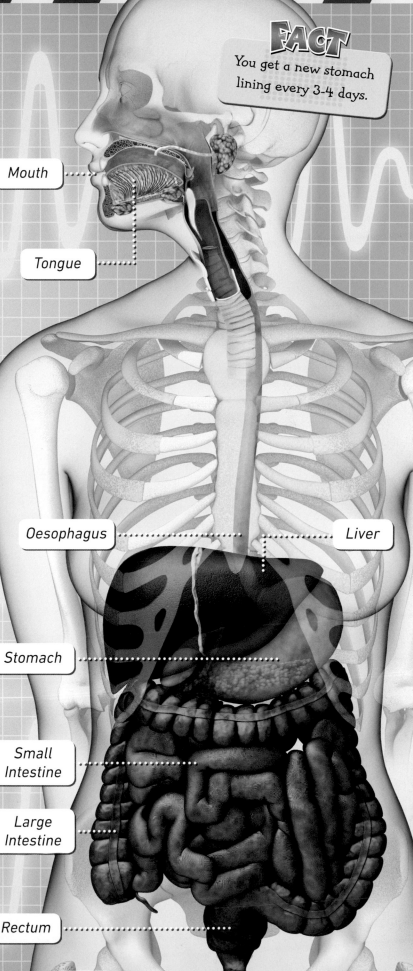

Mouth

Tongue

Oesophagus

Liver

Stomach

Small Intestine

Large Intestine

Rectum

Anus

This Page is Poo!

END OF THE LINE

At the very end of your large intestine is a short tube called your rectum. It's like a waiting-room for poo until it's ready to make an appearance through your anus and into the big wide world. Well, hopefully your toilet.

DID YOU KNOW?

Poo is brown because of the amount of bilirubin it contains. Bilirubin comes from dead red blood cells. The food you eat can also alter the colour of your poo. Things like beetroot or blueberries make a real difference.

FACT
Spread across their lifetime, most people spend an average of one whole year sitting on the toilet.

LOOKING GOOD!

A healthy poo should be shaped like a sausage and be quite squidgy. If it is in separate hard lumps, you may be constipated. And if it is very runny, you probably have diarrhoea which can be caused by an infection or very spicy food.

FRIENDLY FIBRE

High-fibre foods like fruit, vegetables, nuts and bran cereals make it easier to poo. You'll also find that you have more solid, but not hard, poos that glide through your digestive system and land in the toilet with a nice plop. So eating your greens really is important!

FACT
Poos that float have more gas in them.

PLOP!

SITTING AROUND

If you eat foods that are low in fibre, like white rice, cheese and crisps, not only will they take longer to digest in your stomach, but you'll have to sit around and wait longer before your poo makes an appearance.

FACT
The average adult produces around 0.5kg of poo per day.

FACT
More than half your poo is likely to be water.

YUCK!

If you've ever had diarrhoea, you'll know that it's not a very pleasant experience.

A normal poo is solid, whereas diarrhoea is much more runny — sometimes it's virtually like a soupy liquid. One of the most common reasons is if you get a tummy bug and the result is that your body ejects the contents of your digestive system as quickly as possible.

DIY Diarrhoea

NORMAL POO

DIARRHOEA

DID YOU KNOW?

Diarrhoea is much heavier than normal poo because it contains more water.

THE POO FACTORY

Using some food, a potato masher, some old tights, some squeezing, and a hose, Chris and Xand created their very own Poo Factory to show you what goes on in your body to produce a normal poo and diarrhoea.

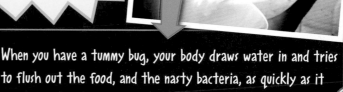

FOOD WAS MASHED UP IN THE MOUTH, REPRESENTED BY A BOWL, READY FOR SWALLOWING.

The tights in the Poo Factory represented the intestines. A rich liquid full of nutrients and water comes out of the intestines and goes into the body, and in the Poo Factory was collected in trays.

When you have a tummy bug, your body draws water in and tries to flush out the food, and the nasty bacteria, as quickly as it can. In the Poo Factory, a hose was used to demonstrate this.

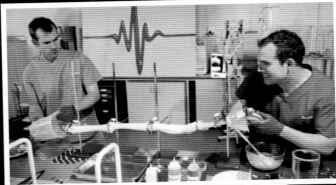

When the food had been processed, nice healthy poo was ejected as a waste product at the end of the line.

When food hasn't been processed correctly, and with all the additional water, a very runny poo is ejected as a waste product at the end of the line.

DON'T TRY THIS AT HOME!

MY BROTHER SWALLOWED A CAMERA

BY XAND VAN TULLEKEN

My brother did something really cool – he swallowed a camera! Not a big camera, but a really small one with lights on and everything!

Doctors use these camera pills to find out what's happening inside people's stomachs. Although it took about eight hours to make it all the way through to Chris' bum (hehehe!), it only took seven seconds to make it to Chris' stomach before we saw an image actually inside his belly! The muscles that push the food through looked like ridges.

CAMERA

STOMACH

CHRIS BODYCAM

For a bit of fun, I decided to feed Chris some jelly-bear sweets to see if they'd show up on the camera in his stomach.

And guess what! They showed up on the camera looking like they were about to give each other a bear-hug!

CHRIS BODYCAM

When the camera (and the sweets) got to the small intestine you could see the furry lining on the walls made up of tiny finger-like things that help to break down food.

LARGE INTESTINE

Next up, the camera bumped into some poo in Chris' large intestine!

I decided to leave Chris to it after it got to that stage!

SMALL INTESTINE   CHRIS BODYCAM

Xand

POO! YUCK!

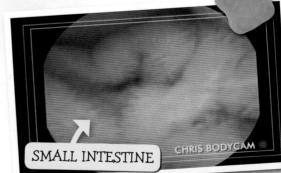

Farty Party

Gross!

Stomach pain is very common. Something that can bring on stomach pain is if you eat your food too fast without chewing it properly. The large chunks are difficult for your stomach to digest. People who wolf down their food often inhale large amounts of air too. All of this leads to an excess of gas to build up in their stomachs.

PARP!

Maybe I should have listened to Mummy van Tulleken after all when she told me to chew my food properly! Xand

FACT

Despite what they say, everyone parps an average of 14 times per day!

FACT

Many people think that methane is the main gas produced in farts. In fact, less than 50% of people make any methane in their farts at all!

Blame the Bacteria!

Inside your large intestines, there are billions of good bacteria working hard to break down the food. As they process the food, they produce a mixture of gases including more methane, carbon dioxide and hydrogen sulphide.

BURP!

So that means that the next time you trump, you can blame it on your stomach bacteria! Chris

FACT

On average you fart enough in one day to fill a party balloon.

The Science of Stinks

The reason some foods make you fart more than others is that they contain particular kinds of sugars that are hard to digest. Those sugars get through your small bowel undigested and end up in your large bowel, where they feed the bacteria. Those bacteria digest them and make gases like carbon dioxide and methane in the process. Certain foods like meat, beans, Brussels sprouts and cauliflower can make for particularly pungent bottom burps!

FACT

Farts have been measured at 7mph!

WHAT HAPPENED TO THE FART WHO MISBEHAVED AT SCHOOL?

I DON'T KNOW

SHE GOT EXPELLED!

OUCH! Take #466:

Mr Methane is someone who has mastered the art of opening up his rear to draw in air and then expel it. It's not actually the same thing as farting, but it's still a neat party trick!

That's Sick!

YUCK!

Sick. Vomit. Puke. Whatever you call it, it's pretty gross stuff. If you've ever looked closely at sick, you'll know that there are often bits of undigested food in there. This is because your stomach isn't choosy about what it brings up. Your body makes you sick because it detects something unpleasant (such as a bacteria or virus) and wants to eject everything as quickly as possible.

CHRIS' SICK

Carrot

Sweetcorn

CHEESY

Some people think that sick smells a bit like cheese. Or that certain cheeses, like parmesan, smell a bit like sick. There's a perfectly good reason for this! When food is broken down in your stomach by bacteria, butyric acid is produced. The same bacterial process occurs when some cheese ages, which is why sick can smell cheesy, and cheese can smell sicky!

So I wonder if you eat some parmesan just before you're sick, you get a doubly cheesy whiff to your vomit? Xand

YOU SPEW, I SPEW, WE ALL SPEW!

Lots of people find that if someone near them is being sick, they need to be sick too. Some scientists think that this could go back to the days when people used to get together to eat in large groups. If one person was sick, it could mean the food was rotten, so everyone else would be sick too to get rid of anything they'd eaten that could upset their stomachs. Of course, they might just be being sick because they're disgusted by all the other sick!

Robo-Puke

When you're sick, so that you don't make a mess everywhere, you might try and do it into a bowl or if you're lucky you might be able to get to the toilet in time and be able to flush it away. With a little help, Xand and I found out that despite your best efforts, sick can travel quite a distance . . . Chris

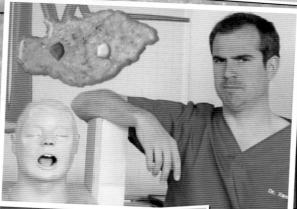

There I was, stood with two dummies — one called Larry and one called Xand. I'm only teasing — Larry isn't a dummy, he's a robot.

I filled up Larry with fake vomit. The liquid contained special fluorescent dye — this will be important in a bit.

WHOA!

LOOK AT LARRY VOMIT!

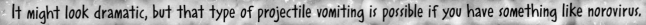

It might look dramatic, but that type of projectile vomiting is possible if you have something like norovirus.

Luckily there was a tray in front of Larry to collect the sick. Well, most of it . . .

Remember the fluorescent dye I mixed in? When we turned off the lights in the lab and used special UV lights, you could see just how far the vomit travelled. Some of it was up to two metres away from Larry! This is why it is very important to make sure all surfaces are properly cleaned after you've been sick, because all of those splatters can spread the virus.

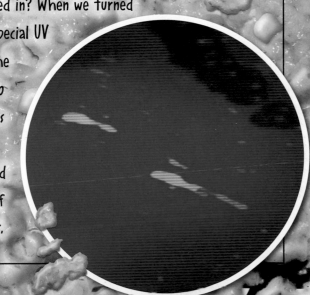

Wee-ly Wonderful!

WATER WORKS

Your body is made up of about 60% water and on average we lose and gain just under three litres per day. Lots of this water comes from the things you drink, but a surprisingly high amount comes from our food too. Water comes out of us in a number of ways like sweating, vapour on our breath and a small amount in our poo. But the majority of it comes out in our wee.

60%

FACT

Wee contains ammonia, which is also used in cleaning products. The ancient Romans even used wee to clean their clothes!

Hmmm, I wonder if wee would work on doctors' scrubs too? I might test it out on Chris' first though!

Xand

PONG!
PONG!
PONG!

COLOUR CHANGER

Have you noticed that your wee can change colour? It can go from being almost clear to an orangey colour. This is all down to how much you drink and how much you sweat. The more water you drink, the clearer your wee will be. If you notice that your wee is looking darker, it could be a sign that you are dehydrated and need to drink more water. Your wee can also look darker when the weather is hot and you haven't been drinking enough extra water to make up for the fluids you are losing through sweat.

DID YOU KNOW?

Weeing is very important because it is a way for our bodies to get rid of poisonous substances.

FACT

Certain foods like asparagus can make your wee smell pretty stinky!

WOW!

Your bladder is small and wrinkled when empty, a bit like a deflated balloon. However, it stretches when it becomes full of wee, but you'll find that it only has space for about 200ml before you start feeling the urge to visit the bathroom. This urge is brought on by sensors in the wall of the bladder that send a message to the brain.

FACT

We wee enough wee every month to fill a bath!

WHAT HAPPENS IF YOU PUT A TOILET ON YOUR HEAD?

I DON'T KNOW

URINE DANGER!

DON'T TRY THIS AT HOME!

DID YOU KNOW?

Your kidneys work hard to get rid of waste products called toxins and hold on to water that's needed to make your body work. Your wee is the mixture of those waste toxins and any leftover water. There's more about how your kidneys work later in this HuManual on pages 112 and 113.

YUCK!

BUT IS IT POSSIBLE TO REMOVE THOSE NASTY TOXINS AND THEN DRINK THE WATER THAT'S LEFT? SOUNDS DISGUSTING, RIGHT?

First up, a sample of wee is necessary

Then in the lab, lots of kit is set up so that the wee can be heated up. This allows water vapour to evaporate and then be cooled in a tube further along the process, resulting in clear water dripping out at the end into a glass!

Amazingly, in just this tiny distance it's possible to go from filthy, disgusting, undrinkable wee to clear water!

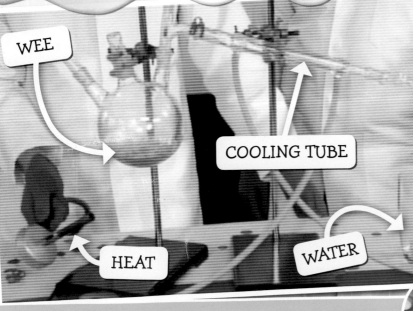

WEE

COOLING TUBE

HEAT

WATER

AND IF YOU'RE WONDERING, THE WATER DIDN'T TASTE TOO BAD AT ALL! BUT IT SMELT REVOLTING!

DEFINITELY DON'T TRY THIS AT HOME! ⚠

Good Poo VS Bad Poo

✓

✗

MADE FROM A HEALTHY DIET, RICH IN FRUIT, VEGETABLES AND FIBRE.

HELPED BY DRINKING LOTS OF WATER.

IT SMELLS, BUT THIS ISN'T A BAD THING! POO SMELLS BECAUSE OF ALL THE BACTERIA IN YOUR DIGESTIVE SYSTEM. AS EVERYTHING GETS BROKEN DOWN THEY RELEASE A LOT OF GAS AND SMELLY CHEMICALS.

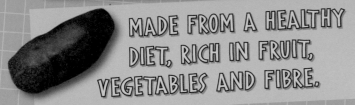

FIBRE MAKES YOUR POO SOLID AND DRINKING LOTS OF WATER HELPS YOUR POO GLIDE THROUGH YOUR LARGE INTESTINE BETTER TOO.

MADE FROM AN UNHEALTHY DIET OF SWEET AND DEEP-FRIED FOODS.

VERY LITTLE WATER DRUNK, MAKING THE BODY, AND THE POO, DEHYDRATED.

SMALL, DRY, HARD AND SMELLS VERY BAD.

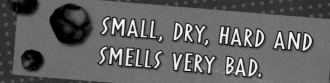

JUNK FOOD IS FULL OF FATS AND SUGARS BUT VERY LITTLE FIBRE, SO YOUR GUTS FIND IT HARDER TO PUSH THROUGH AND IT SITS THERE FOR AGES, MAKING YOU CONSTIPATED.

PICK a POO

WELCOME TO THE PICK A POO SUPERMARKET!

SELECT WHICH FOODS BELONG IN WHICH TROLLEY TO GIVE YOU HEALTHY POO, DIARRHOEA AND CONSTIPATION.

NASTY BACTERIA

HEALTHY POO

DIARRHOEA

CONSTIPATION

PANCREAS POWER

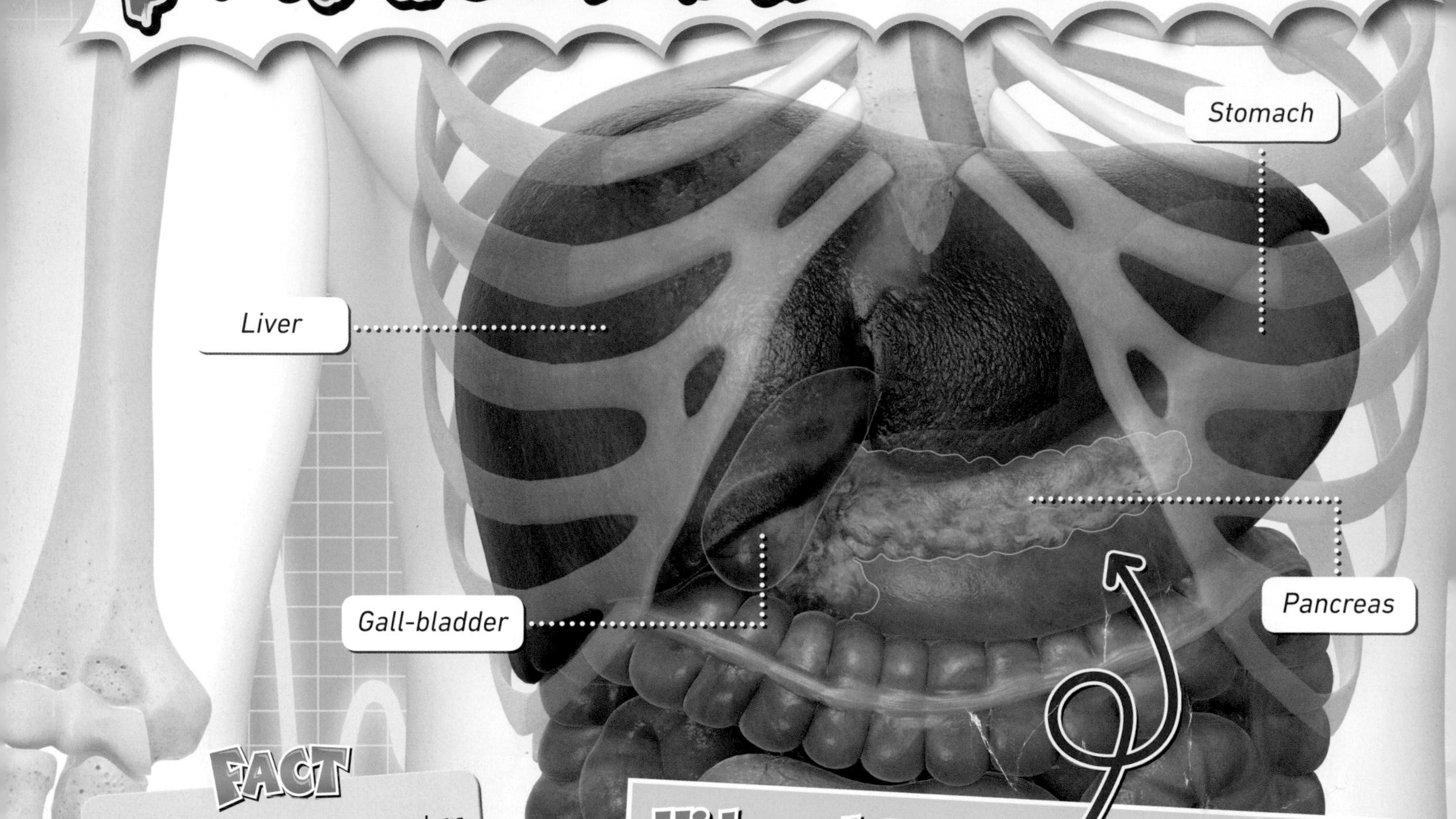

Stomach

Liver

Gall-bladder

Pancreas

FACT

Your pancreas has taste receptors similar to your tongue. When the pancreas tastes fructose in your food, it responds by producing more insulin.

Hide and Seek

Your pancreas is hidden between other organs. It is a long organ that runs horizontally between your stomach and your spine, and is connected to the first section of the small intestine which is looped around it.

Silent Hero

Your pancreas probably isn't on many people's list of favourite parts of the body. It doesn't get the same amount of attention as things like the heart, brain or lungs. However, it is a vital part of your anatomy and worth a look.

Maybe we need to start the Pancreases Are Nice Terrific Specimens club! Actually, that would make it the P.A.N.T.S. club – I'll work on the name! Xand

Hard Worker

Food that has been partially digested by the stomach arrives at the pancreas and pancreatic juice is released. This juice contains enzymes that digest proteins, carbohydrates and nucleic acids. With the help of a yellow liquid called bile, which is released by your gall-bladder, another enzyme digests the fats in your food. Your body is then able to absorb all of these nutrients and put them to work!

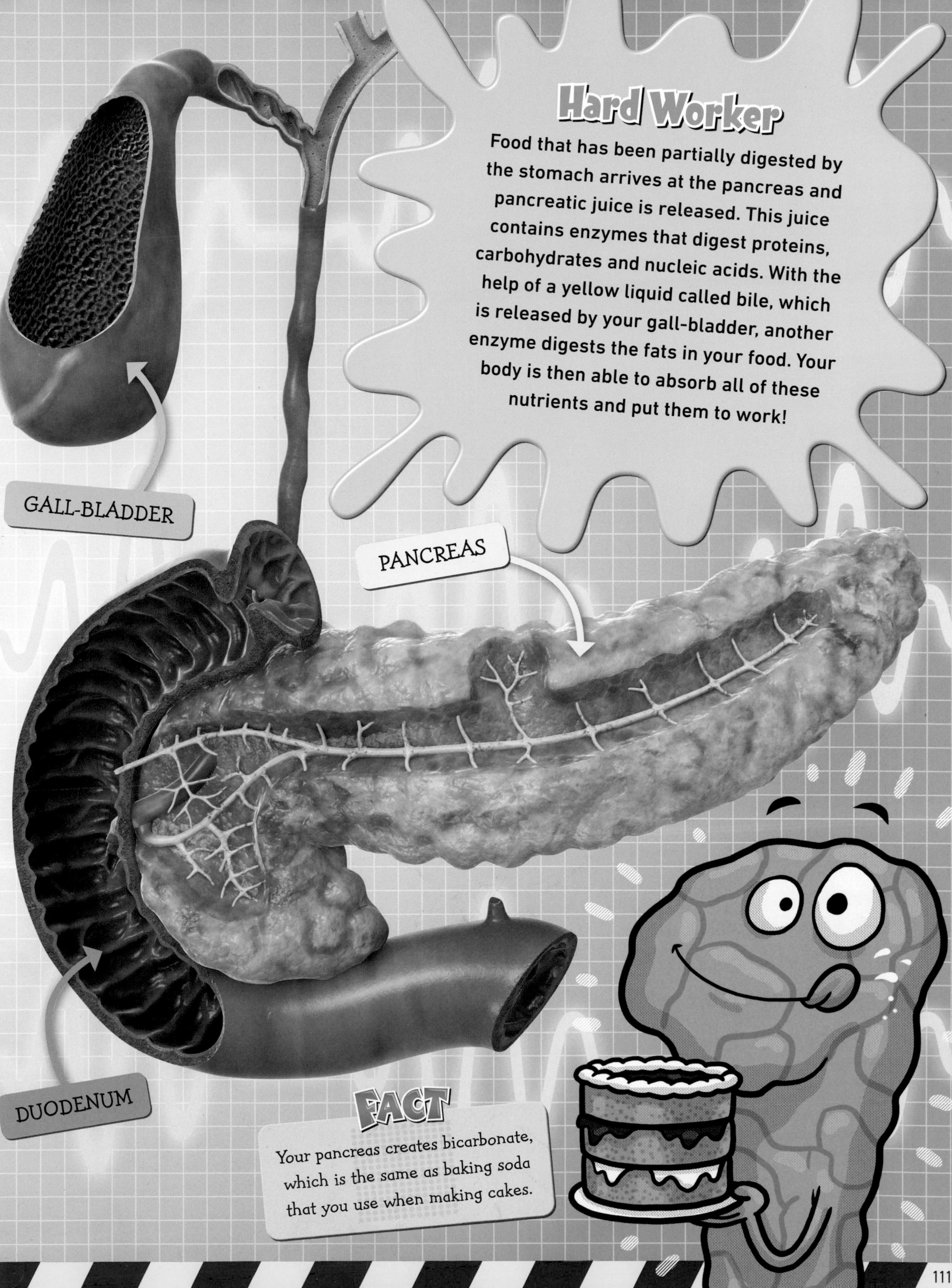

GALL-BLADDER

PANCREAS

DUODENUM

FACT

Your pancreas creates bicarbonate, which is the same as baking soda that you use when making cakes.

KIDNEYS MAKE

WEES!

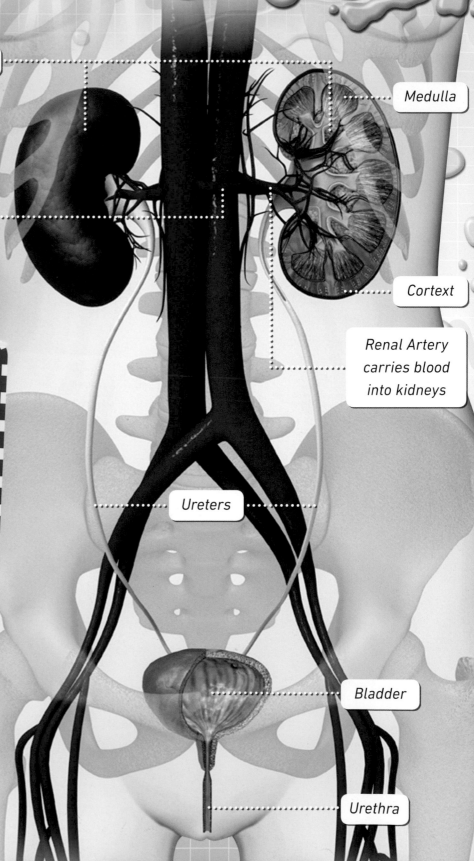

FACT

In 24 hours your kidneys filter and clean 200 litres of blood.

Renal Vein carries clean blood from kidneys

DID YOU KNOW?

Your body is full of waste products that need to be collected and disposed of – a bit like putting out the rubbish. Your urinary system plays a key role in this process by eliminating waste and removing excess water and salts from your blood. Along with two ureters, the bladder and the urethra, your two kidneys make up your urinary system.

FACT

Each kidney is about the size of a computer mouse.

Kidney

Medulla

Cortext

Renal Artery carries blood into kidneys

Ureters

Bladder

Urethra

Looks Familiar

If you've ever eaten a chilli con carne, the shape and name of one of your kidneys might be familiar. This is because kidney beans resemble the shape and colour of the organ in your body.

First wees, now chilli con carne — I don't know if I want to visit the bathroom or the kitchen! Xand

AW, THEY'RE SO CUTE!

Urine for a Treat!

The kidneys filter and clean blood that's received through the renal artery, leaving you with wee ready to travel along a tube called the ureter and into your bladder.

OUCH! Take #118:

Cleaning time! Each kidney has an outer region that contains one million filtration units called nephrons. Inside the nephrons, fluid is filtered from the blood to separate good substances from waste substances. The useful substances are sent back into the blood, whilst the bad substances head off for disposal.

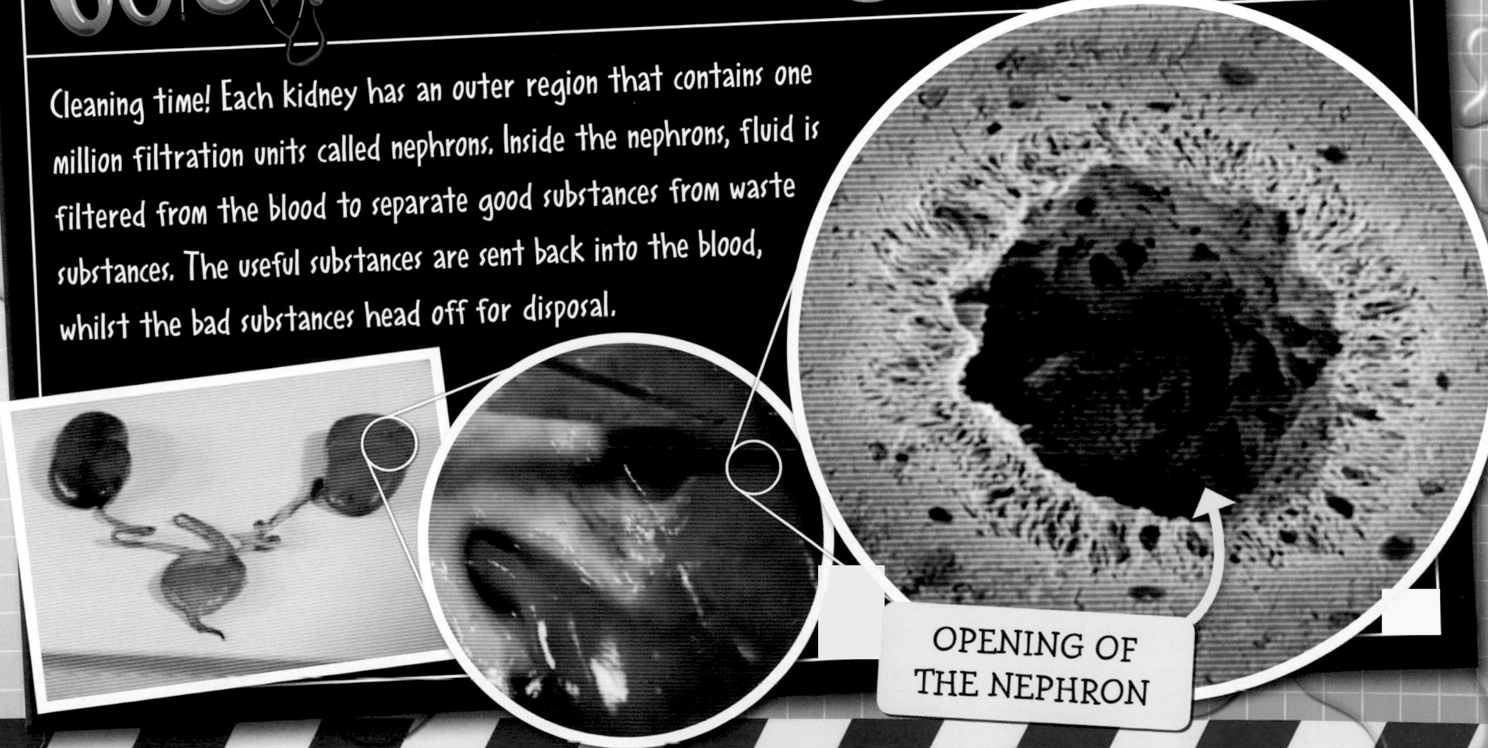

OPENING OF THE NEPHRON

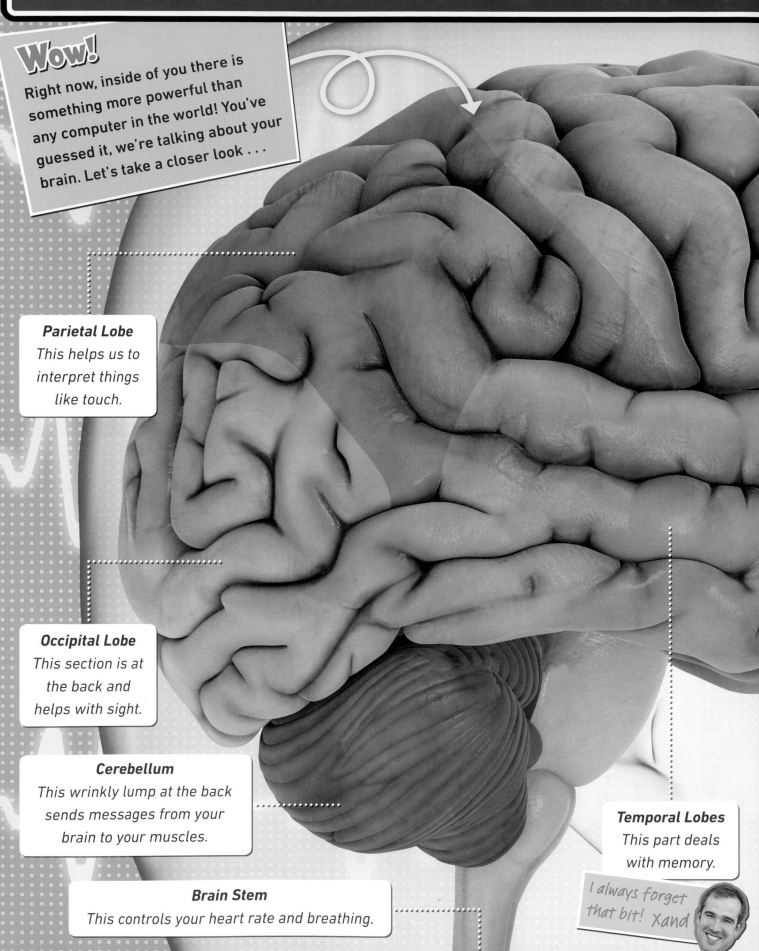

Wow!

Right now, inside of you there is something more powerful than any computer in the world! You've guessed it, we're talking about your brain. Let's take a closer look . . .

Parietal Lobe
This helps us to interpret things like touch.

Occipital Lobe
This section is at the back and helps with sight.

Cerebellum
This wrinkly lump at the back sends messages from your brain to your muscles.

Temporal Lobes
This part deals with memory.

I always forget that bit! Xand

Brain Stem
This controls your heart rate and breathing.

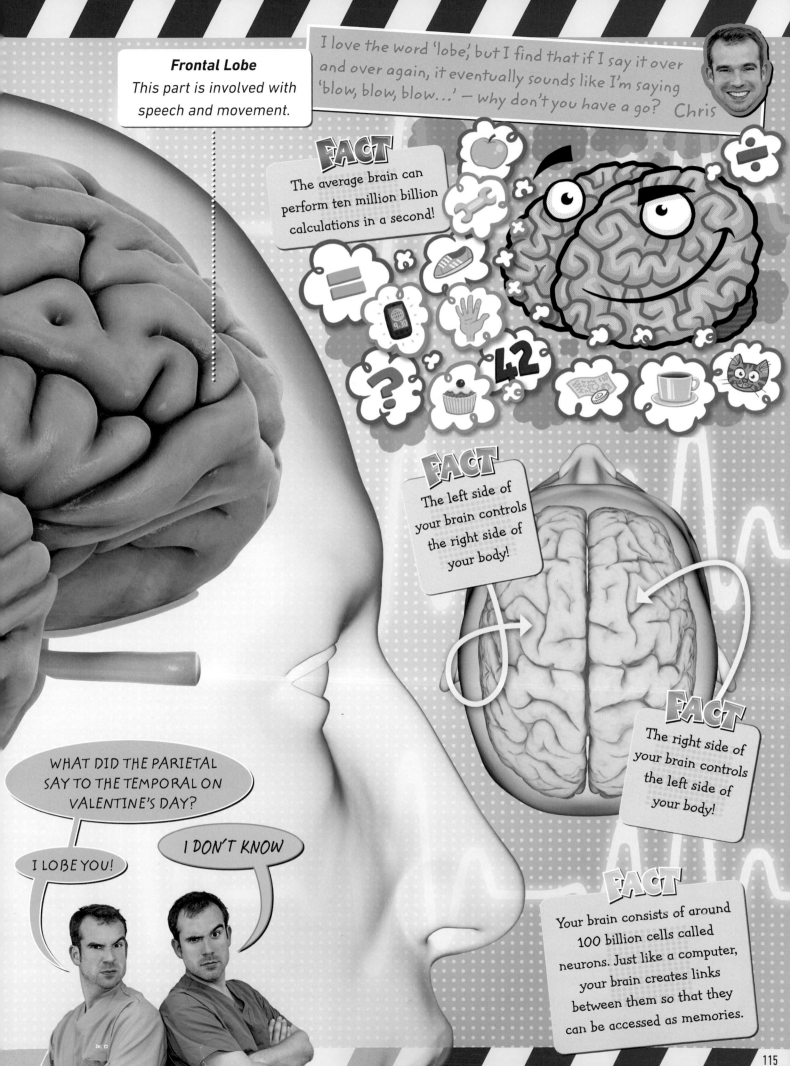

Frontal Lobe
This part is involved with speech and movement.

I love the word 'lobe,' but I find that if I say it over and over again, it eventually sounds like I'm saying 'blow, blow, blow...' — why don't you have a go?   Chris

FACT
The average brain can perform ten million billion calculations in a second!

FACT
The left side of your brain controls the right side of your body!

FACT
The right side of your brain controls the left side of your body!

WHAT DID THE PARIETAL SAY TO THE TEMPORAL ON VALENTINE'S DAY?

I LOBE YOU!

I DON'T KNOW

FACT
Your brain consists of around 100 billion cells called neurons. Just like a computer, your brain creates links between them so that they can be accessed as memories.

Knock, Knock

FACT
Your cerebrum makes up the vast majority of your brain and has a wrinkly surface, and is what most people picture when they think of a brain.

Take Care!

Your brain may be an amazingly complicated, impressive machine, but it is also very fragile and needs to be protected from knocks. Your brain is basically a soft, floppy, squidgy organ that is extremely delicate.

There's More!

Between the brain and skull are soft membranes and a cushioning fluid (called cerebrospinal fluid) which help to protect everything even more, which is good because keeping your brain safe is a big priority for your body!

FACT
The weight of the brain in average adult males is 1375 grammes, while in females it is 1275 grammes.

Hair to Help

Externally you have skin and hair that help protect the brain even more. However, you may find that you need to wear a helmet or hard hat when doing certain sports, activities or jobs to be extra safe.

DID YOU KNOW?
The brain is protected by a hard bone called the skull (there's more about this on page 46). The part of the skull responsible for looking after the brain is called the cranium and is made of eight cranial bones. The cranium is thin but super-strong.

Ouch!

You might have heard of something called a concussion. The medical term is: a minor traumatic brain injury, which helps a bit to explain what it is. A serious hit to the head can hurt your brain and temporarily change the way your brain works. If that happens, the brain injury is called a concussion. If your head is hit hard enough, the brain can shift inside of the skull and knock against the bony surface of the skull. If you or a friend has a knock to the head, it's always a good idea to let an adult know and seek medical attention if there's any doubt.

FACT
Your brain consumes 20% of the body's energy, despite making up only 2% of its weight.

Amazing Maze

YOUR BRAIN IS AN AMAZING PART OF YOUR BODY. BUT CAN YOU SOLVE THIS MAZE AND MAKE IT FROM YOUR CEREBRUM TO YOUR SPINAL CORD?

START

FINISH

MEMORY

DID YOU KNOW?

There isn't just one part of your brain that is used to store memories. Lots of bits work together, like the cerebral cortex and hippocampus, to help you remember things.

Cerebral Cortex

Hippocampus

Sensory Memory

This type of memory deals with everything that is happening around you. Some of it is only analysed and stored for a split second because your brain doesn't think that it is important enough to go into your short-term memory. Just think, if your brain remembered every little sight, sound, taste, touch it would soon become overwhelmed.

Short-term Memory

Only significant sensations are remembered thanks to your short-term memory. It allows you to recall things for a short period of time, sometimes only for a few seconds, so that you can respond to them. More important things are logged in your long-term memory.

Procedural Memory

This is a type of long-term memory and allows you to remember how to do certain skills that you have learnt, like walking or riding a bike. These skills are difficult to forget and even if you haven't done something in a while, your brain soon remembers, which is where the phrase 'you never forget, like riding a bike' comes from.

Episodic Memory

Remember that great holiday you had? Or your first day at school? How about that trip to the dentist? That's all because of your long-term episodic memory which allows you to recall specific events. Sometimes looking back through old photographs can help trigger this part of your brain.

FACT A rough calculation by Paul Reber, Professor of Psychology at Northwestern University in the USA suggested that the brain can store 2.5 petabytes of data – that's 2,500,000 gigabytes, or 300 years' worth of non-stop, 24-hour-a-day TV!

Semantic Memory

This part of your long-term memory allows you to recall how to read, speak and remember facts. Which is pretty useful or you wouldn't be able to understand this HuManual!

Memory Test

HOW GOOD IS YOUR SHORT-TERM MEMORY? IT'S TIME TO PUT IT TO THE TEST!

Look at the objects below for 30 seconds (either set a countdown timer or ask someone to time you). Then, close the book and try to write down as many of the objects as you can.

MY MEMORY IS SO BAD!

HOW BAD IS IT?

HOW BAD IS WHAT?

YOU CAN TRY IT OUT ON YOUR FRIENDS AND FAMILY TOO AND SEE HOW WELL THEY DO!

THE BRAIN SCRAMBLER

There are three things I love – nose-picking, playing with amazing bits of technology and making Chris look silly. Luckily the day I brought a Brain Scrambler into the lab, I was able to do all three! Xand

To demonstrate that your brain uses electrical signals to tell different parts of your body what to do, I borrowed Chris' head.

I then got hold of a multipulse transcranial magnetic stimulator, or as I like to call it, a Brain Scrambler! Basically, a giant magnet.

I placed the magnet on the right side of Chris' head and asked him to pick his left nostril with his left hand.

And this is how he got on! Despite nose-picking being something I know he does all the time, he was unable to do this simple action when I switched on →  THE BRAIN SCRAMBLER

This is because your brain is actually wired back to front, so the right side of the brain controls the left side of the body. The magnets altered the electrical signals that Chris' brain was sending. Nose-picking, the Brain Scrambler, and Chris looking silly – what's not to love?!

DO TRY THIS AT HOME!

WHILST MOST PEOPLE DON'T HAVE A MULTIPULSE TRANSCRANIAL MAGNETIC STIMULATOR LIKE XAND, HERE'S A TRICK THAT YOU CAN USE TO SCRAMBLE YOUR FRIENDS' BRAINS THAT DOESN'T REQUIRE ANY EQUIPMENT OTHER THAN A NORMAL CHAIR!

First, tell your friend to sit in a chair, raise their right foot and move it in a clockwise circle.

Then, whilst they are doing this, ask them to trace a number six in the air with their right index finger.

THEY WON'T BE ABLE TO DO BOTH MOVEMENTS AT ONCE — **BRAIN SCRAMBLE!**

Why does this work?

The parts of your brain that control movement can't deal with two opposite movements happening at the same time. With their foot going clockwise and their finger moving anticlockwise, their brain becomes so confused it starts trying to make both their foot and their finger move in the same direction.

GET ON YOUR NERVES →

Wow!

As you know, your brain is located in your head, and from here it is able to control your whole body. It does this through a network of nerves that link your brain to all the different parts of your body — they are a bit like cables and wires that send information. Together they make up your Nervous System.

Working 24/7

It might sound complicated, but your nervous system works 24 hours a day, constantly monitoring what is going on and sending messages around the body. It's an expert at multi-tasking and works without you even having to think about it.

If it works 24/7, I wonder what happens when your nervous system wants to go on its summer holidays? Chris

DID YOU KNOW?

Your cranial nerves join places like your eyes, ears, nose, tongue, lungs and heart to your brain. Your spinal cord links your brain to other parts of your body. The brain and spinal cord make up your central nervous system and are responsible for lots of things you do all the time like chatting to your mates and eating your lunch. Leading from your spinal cord are pairs of smaller nerves that link to your muscles, blood vessels and other body parts.

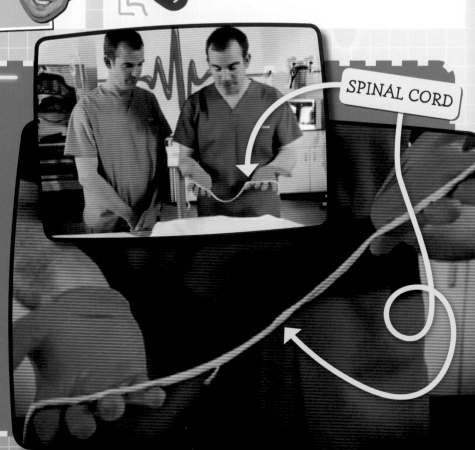

SPINAL CORD

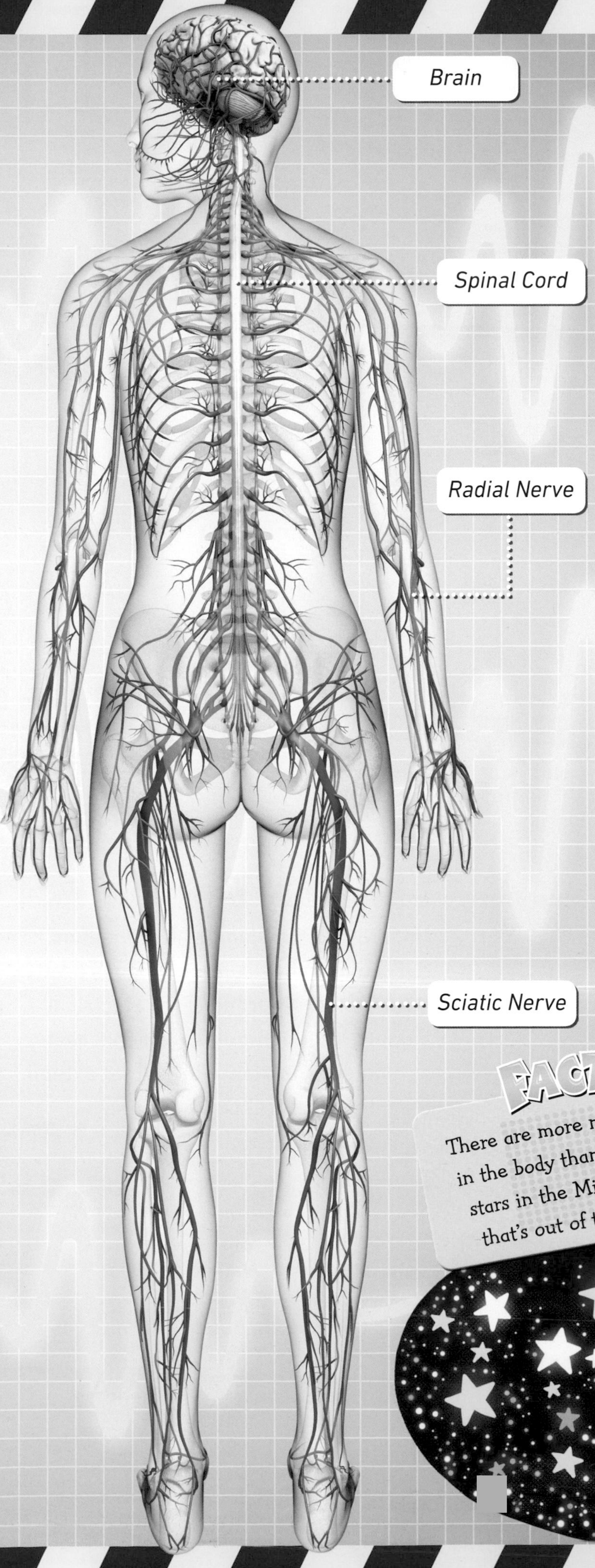

Brain

Spinal Cord

Radial Nerve

Sciatic Nerve

Ouch!

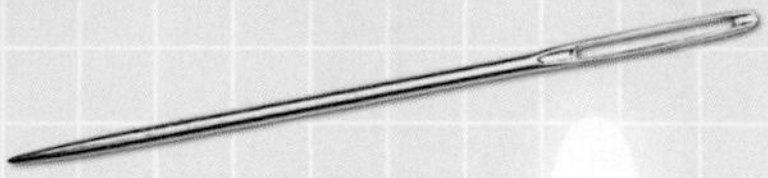

You have probably experienced the minor nerve condition called paraesthesia at some point. It's better known as pins and needles and is the tingly, prickly, numb feeling you get when you do something like stand up after you've been kneeling down for a long time. It is caused by the temporary cutting-off of the blood supply to your nerves, in this case in your lower legs and feet. The pins and needles sensation is actually when the blood rushes back to the nerves and they start working again. It's nothing to worry about and usually goes quite quickly.

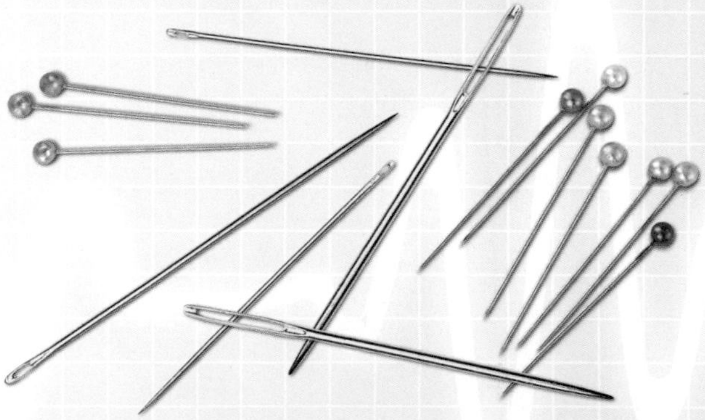

So although pins and needles can feel quite uncomfortable, even a bit scary, it's just your blood getting back to where it should be! Chris

FACT

There are more nerve cells in the body than there are stars in the Milky Way — that's out of this world!

The Nerve of It

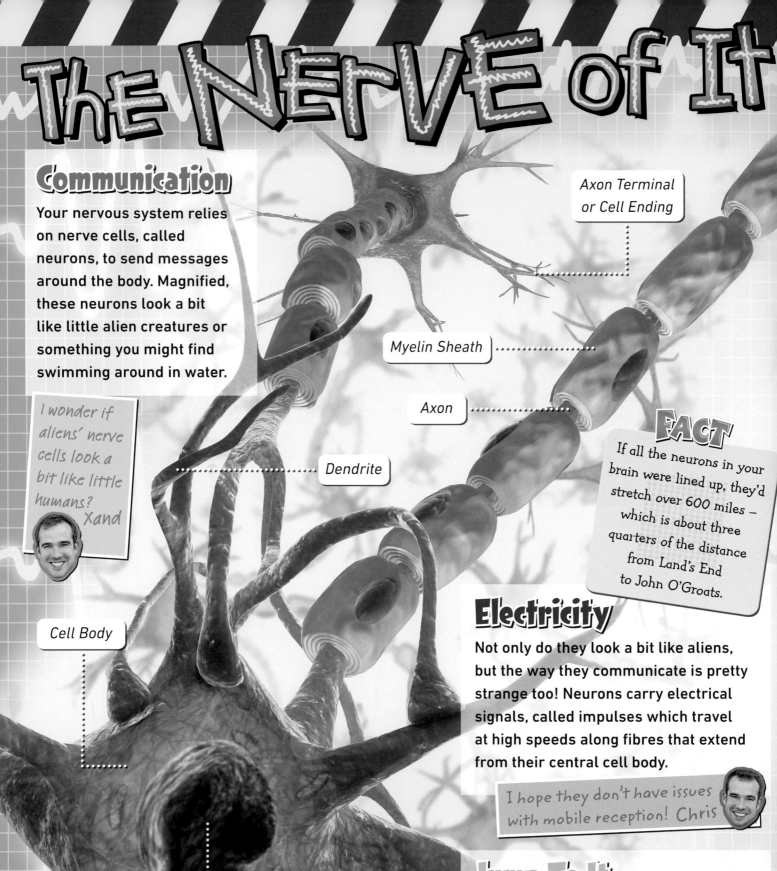

Communication

Your nervous system relies on nerve cells, called neurons, to send messages around the body. Magnified, these neurons look a bit like little alien creatures or something you might find swimming around in water.

I wonder if aliens' nerve cells look a bit like little humans? Xand

Axon Terminal or Cell Ending

Myelin Sheath

Axon

Dendrite

Cell Body

Nucleus

FACT
If all the neurons in your brain were lined up, they'd stretch over 600 miles – which is about three quarters of the distance from Land's End to John O'Groats.

FACT
There are approximately 100 billion neurons in the brain, and a further 13.5 million in the spinal cord.

Electricity

Not only do they look a bit like aliens, but the way they communicate is pretty strange too! Neurons carry electrical signals, called impulses which travel at high speeds along fibres that extend from their central cell body.

I hope they don't have issues with mobile reception! Chris

Jump To It

Impulses jump between neurons, so that they can pass on and receive information – it's a bit like sending each other text messages! The process of an impulse going from one neuron to another is called neurotransmission.

Tea Time

WELCOME TO THE OPERATION OUCH! TEA SHOP! BUT IT'S A TEA SHOP WITH A DIFFERENCE . . .

At one end is Chris who represents a brain. He wants a cup of tea so has to send a message down a nerve through the neurons to his hand, represented by Xand. Let's see how they get on . . .

Sending this message up and down the queue between the brain and the hand took quite a while. But luckily your nervous system is able to do this quickly. Very quickly. This whole process of deciding to have a cup of tea, picking it up, realizing it was too hot and putting it back down actually goes at speeds of 100 metres per second!

100

125

Responses

Auto Response

Blinking, sneezing, yawning, pulling your finger away quickly from something hot. All of these things happen without our actually thinking about it, don't they? This happens because the spinal cord is able to send messages to the muscles without even involving the brain. We call these reflexes.

I sometimes think that Xand is like a reflex — he has the ability to irritate me without even thinking about it! Chris

Ouch!

Pain receptors in our skin generate nerve impulses causing us to react straight away to even the smallest pain, like the prick of a pin on your fingertip.

Knees Up

If there was a Top 10 chart for the most famous reflex, the knee-jerk one (called the patellar reflex) would come pretty high up. You've probably seen it – it's when a doctor taps the area just below a patient's kneecap to make the lower leg jolt up.

DID YOU KNOW?

Babies are born with reflexes that help them survive. The sucking reflex happens automatically so that they can drink milk. Babies turn their head when the side of their face is touched so that they are in the right position to feed – this is called the rooting reflex. Babies are also able to hold their breath and make swimming movements underwater. But the reason you've had to learn to swim from scratch is that you lose these reflexes by the time you are one year old!

Reflex Race

TRY OUT THIS REFLEX RACE ON SOMEONE TO MEASURE THEIR RESPONSE TO SOMETHING THAT THEY SEE. THEN GET THEM TO TRY IT ON YOU AND COMPARE RESULTS.

1. Grab a 30cm ruler.

2. Hold it at the end where the number is highest and let it hang down.

3. Tell the person you're testing to place their thumb and forefinger at the other end, hovering over the 0cm mark, but without actually touching the ruler.

4. Then tell them that within five seconds you will drop the ruler and they must catch it between their thumb and forefinger.

5. Within five seconds, drop the ruler.

6. When you have done this, make a note of how far up their thumb and forefinger caught the ruler.

7. If you want to be really accurate, try it a few times.

8. You can then work out their reaction time using the table below – for example, if their thumb and forefinger caught the ruler at the 10cm mark, their reaction time would be 0.14 seconds.

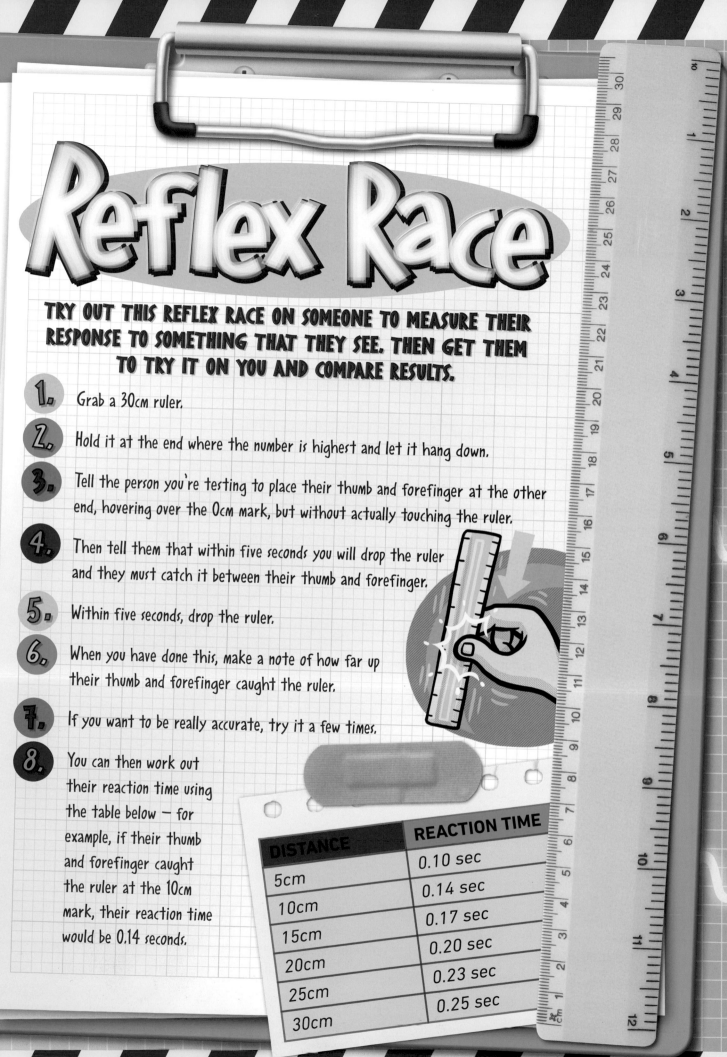

DISTANCE	REACTION TIME
5cm	0.10 sec
10cm	0.14 sec
15cm	0.17 sec
20cm	0.20 sec
25cm	0.23 sec
30cm	0.25 sec

BEDTIME →

Housekeeping

Sleep is a time for your body to make sure that everything is OK and mend any cells that might need to be repaired or fixed.

Zzzzzz

Everyone needs sleep. Although it might seem like your body is switched off when you fall asleep, there's actually still quite a lot going on.

And Relax . . .

Muscles in places like your neck, back and legs work hard during the day. They work to support your body and keep you upright. However, when you sleep, your muscles are able to relax. This is why your body becomes floppy when you sleep or if you fall asleep in a chair, your head might loll forwards or to the side.

Down Time

When we're asleep, our brains are given time to process the experiences of the past day. It is also able to file certain events away in our memories. It's a bit like doing a computer back-up.

FACT

On average, we spend a third of our lives sleeping.

DID YOU KNOW?

There are different 'stages' of sleep. Soon after you fall asleep, you experience something called non-rapid eye movement (NREM), when your brain activity decreases sharply. Next is a phase of rapid eye movement (REM), when although you are asleep your brain becomes active and you dream. Your eyes may flicker, but your eyelids remain closed and the other muscles in your body don't move. This cycle of NREM and REM sleep repeats three or four times throughout the night until you wake up.

Who knew there was so much going on when you sleep? It's so exhausting, it's making me feel a bit sleepy... Zzzzzz... Chris

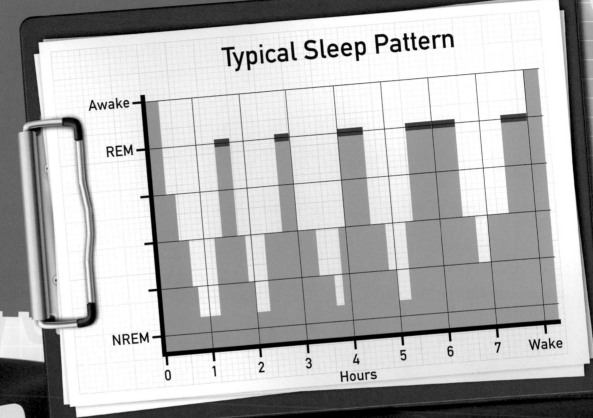

Typical Sleep Pattern

Awake
REM
NREM
Wake

0   1   2   3   4   5   6   7

Hours

FACT

Newborn babies sleep for about 20 hours per day.

FACT

Most adults need between about seven and eight hours' sleep a night.

REALLY

I DON'T UNDERSTAND PEOPLE WHO HAVE TROUBLE SLEEPING

YES, I CAN DO IT WITH MY EYES CLOSED!

Feeling Sleepy

YAWN!

Open Wide

You may have noticed that when you are tired, your mouth opens wide and a deep breath is taken in. You guessed it – this is called yawning.

It's a Mystery

Yawning can happen when we are tired or bored, but exactly why we yawn is still a bit of a mystery, even to doctors. Some people think that it might be to quickly release large amounts of carbon dioxide and take in more oxygen to help keep you awake. Others think it could be used to cool down your brain. It's even been suggested that it developed as a means of communication before we had speech to let other people know we were tired.

CO_2 CO_2 CO_2 CO_2 CO_2 CO_2 CO_2 CO_2 CO_2 CO_2 CO_2 CO_2 CO_2 CO_2 CO_2

One thing that is for certain, it's polite to cover your mouth when you yawn – Mummy van Tulleken taught me that! Xand

DOCTOR XAND, DOCTOR XAND, I CAN'T GET TO SLEEP AT NIGHT

LIE ON THE EDGE OF THE BED AND YOU'LL SOON DROP OFF!

Yawn

72

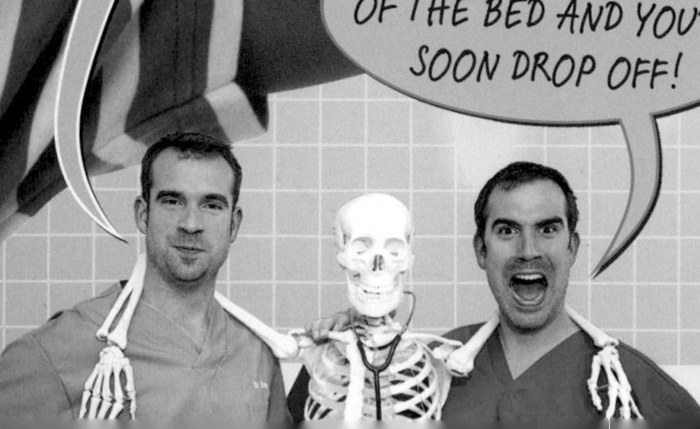

DO TRY THIS AT HOME!

ALTHOUGH WE DON'T KNOW EXACTLY WHY WE YAWN, WHAT WE DO KNOW IS THAT YAWNING CAN BE CONTAGIOUS.

WHY DON'T YOU HAVE A GO!

The next time you're with a group of people — it could be your friends or your family — do a yawn and see if anyone else starts yawning too.

Just don't try it during class or you might get into trouble! Chris

CHRIS AND XAND ASKED SOME OF YOU WHY YOU THINK WE YAWN. HERE'S A COUPLE OF YOUR SUGGESTIONS. ADD IN YOUR OWN SUGGESTION IN THE BLANK SPACE!

I think yawning is a contagious disease, because when one person does it another person does it, then another person does it, and it just keeps on going.

We see someone looking tired and we think, 'I must be tired' because they look tired.

BODY TALK →

The speed that you blink can be used to reveal whether you are telling the truth. The normal blinking rate is 6–8 times per minute, but it often increases when people lie or are under stress.

DID YOU KNOW?

We communicate with each other all the time. The most obvious form of communication is speech, but did you know that we can 'say' things to people without speaking? More than 30 muscles in your face help you make different expressions that show emotions including happiness, sadness, surprise, fear, anger and disgust.

Just like the emoticons you might send in a text message! Chris

Frontalis

Orbicularis Oculi

Levator Labii Superioris

Orbicularis Oris

Secret Signals

The way we position our bodies can also let people know how we are feeling. Sometimes you might not even be aware that you are sending these signals. If you angle your body towards someone, it could be a sign that you like them or trust them, whereas if you angle your body away, it might be because you are wary of them. Or if you sit with your arms folded, this could be seen as a defensive signal and suggest that you don't like someone or you're shy.

Zygomaticus

Depressor Labii Inferioris

Depressor Anguli Oris

FACT

It is estimated that up to 65% of human communication is non-verbal.

132

Pulling Faces

HERE ARE THE SIX BASIC EMOTIONS YOU SHOW ON YOUR FACE AND THE FACIAL MUSCLES YOU USE TO MAKE THEM:

Emotion: **HAPPINESS**

Signs: Big smile, raised cheeks, wrinkles around eyes

Muscles used: Zygomaticus, levator labii superioris

Emotion: **SADNESS**

Signs: Mouth closed and turned down at edges, eyebrows raised in centre

Muscles used: Orbicularis oris, depressor anguli oris, orbicularis oculi

Emotion: **SURPRISE**

Signs: Raised eyebrows, wrinkled forehead, eyes wide open, jaw dropped

Muscles used: Frontalis

Emotion: **FEAR**

Signs: Wrinkled forehead, eyebrows lifted, eyes open wide, lower lip pulled downwards, face becomes paler as blood moves from skin to muscles

Muscles used: Frontalis, depressor labii inferioris

Emotion: **ANGER**

Signs: Eyebrows pulled downwards with wrinkle between them, eyes narrow, teeth exposed

Muscles used: Orbicularis oculi

Emotion: **DISGUST**

Signs: Eyebrows raised in centre, eyes narrowed, tongue sticking out

Muscles used: Orbicularis oris, depressor anguli oris

HOORAY for Hormones

Hypothalamus

Pineal Gland

DID YOU KNOW?

Your body actually has two ways of getting messages around itself. The nervous system sends electrical signals really quickly, while the second system works at a slower pace. This other system is called your endocrine, or hormonal, system.

PINEAL GLAND
This gland is found deep inside your brain and helps to control sleep.

So sleep's not just controlled by closing your curtains and turning off the light!
Chris

SMS (Secret Message Service)

The endocrine system works by releasing chemical messages from things called glands. These messages are then dispatched via your blood to specific cells or tissues with an instruction. These messages are called hormones. And just like you might delete texts when they've been sent, when these messages have been delivered, they are destroyed by your liver.

I always delete my texts because a certain person whose name begins with 'Chr–' and ends in '–is' has a habit of nosing at my phone! Xand

ADRENAL GLANDS
Hormones are released from the outer part of each adrenal gland, whereas the inner part works with your automatic nervous system to release a hormone called adrenalin. You might have heard of adrenalin – it supplies your body with a 'rush' by increasing your heart rate and making you breathe faster to prepare for danger or activity.

Adrenal Glands

OVARIES – Girls Only!
The ovaries play a role in the female endocrine system by producing two hormones called oestrogen and progesterone. Oestrogen is what signals for a girl's body to get breasts, and it also works with progesterone to control the menstrual cycle. There's more about this on page 147.

Ovaries

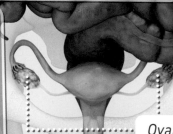

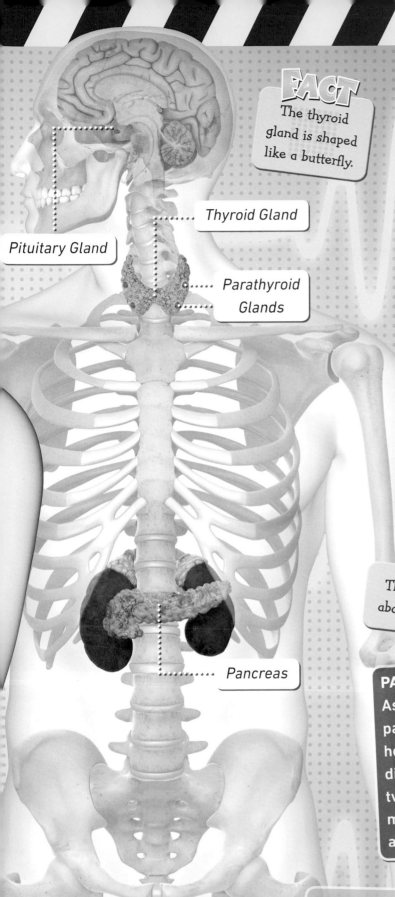

Pituitary Gland

Thyroid Gland

FACT
The thyroid gland is shaped like a butterfly.

Parathyroid Glands

Pancreas

Testes

Control Stations

Different hormones are created in different parts of the body. These glands, which are like control stations, send out specific messages, targeted at certain parts of your body. The glands are the same in males and females, except for the testes that are male only and ovaries that are female only.

PITUITARY GLAND

This gland releases hormones that help with your growth, metabolic rate and reproduction. The pituitary gland is controlled by the brain's hypothalamus.

FACT
The pituitary gland is about the size of a pea.

PANCREAS

As if there weren't enough reasons to love your pancreas on pages 110 and 111 of this HuManual, here's another! Not only does it play a role in the digestive system, but it also works hard releasing two hormones, insulin and glucagon, which help to make sure that your body's energy supply is kept at a pretty constant level in your bloodstream.

TESTES – Boys Only!

The testes release the male sex hormone testosterone. This hormone helps maintain male features like a deep voice, body and facial hair, as well as stimulating sperm production. Check out page 146 for more info.

NICE GENES!

Wow!

Do you remember back at the beginning of this book when we said that your body doesn't come with a set of instructions? Well, that isn't entirely true. Every single part of what makes you you, is determined by a set of instructions inside your body, called your genes. However, they aren't very easy to read from the outside, so there's still a use for your HuManual!

DNA

FACT
The DNA sequences of a few people, including scientist Stephen Hawking, are stored on the International Space Station. They're there to help rebuild the human race if the Earth is destroyed.

I'm still waiting for the call to send some of mine!
Chris

Cell

Chromosome

FACT
If you unravelled all the DNA in your body, it would reach to the moon 6,000 times!

DNA

Jeans

Monkey Business

Humans and chimpanzees actually share 95% of the same DNA.

I reckon Chris is closer to 96% chimp — there's something about the way he eats bananas! Xand

DID YOU KNOW?
Everything about you, from the colour of your skin to whether you're a boy or a girl, comes from your cells. This information is stored on tiny ladder-shaped strands called DNA.

FACT
DNA stands for deoxyribonucleic acid.

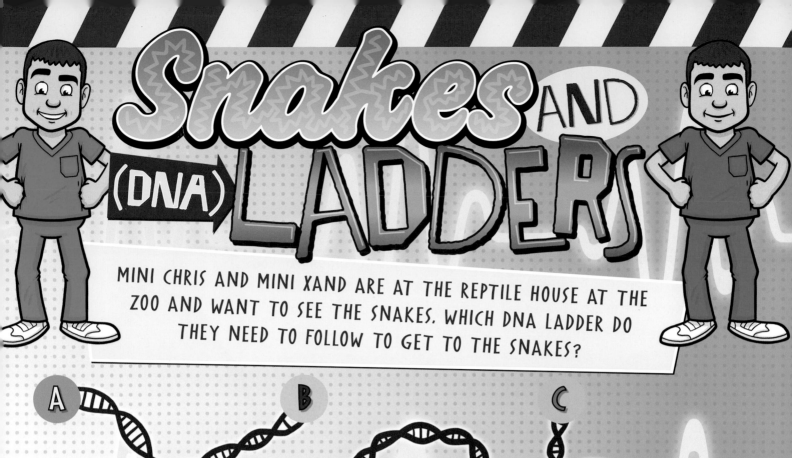

Snakes AND (DNA) LADDERS

MINI CHRIS AND MINI XAND ARE AT THE REPTILE HOUSE AT THE ZOO AND WANT TO SEE THE SNAKES. WHICH DNA LADDER DO THEY NEED TO FOLLOW TO GET TO THE SNAKES?

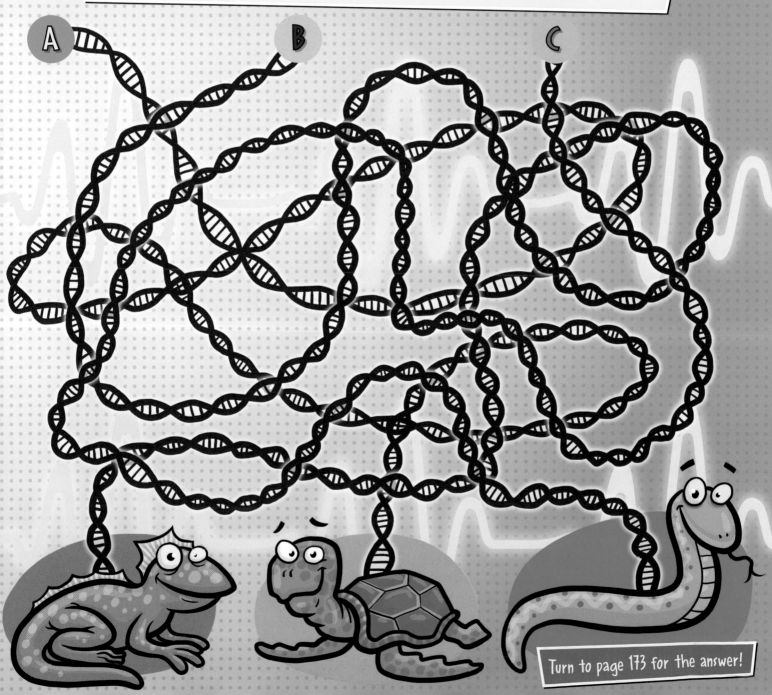

A B C

Turn to page 173 for the answer!

Familiar Faces

X, Y and No Z

Things called chromosomes contain all of the information used to help a cell grow, thrive and reproduce. We all get 23 chromosomes from our mother and 23 from our father. These are grouped into pairs that are numbered from 1 to 22, plus an extra pair called the 'X/Y' pair. The X/Y pair determines if you are a boy or a girl.

I wonder why they chose the letters X and Y? Obviously X is a very cool letter, with lots of great things beginning with an X like my name, but why Y? Xand

Very good, Xand . . . it's simply because the Y is after X in the alphabet and the person that named it thought that made sense!
Chris

DID YOU KNOW?

If you looked at a group of people in a shopping centre or a crowd at a football stadium, you might think that they were all quite different. However, any two people in a crowd will share 99.9% of their DNA. When it comes to members of the same family, this increases to 99.95%! Maybe we aren't all so different after all.

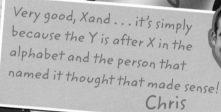

Family Tree

In a family photo, you can often see that the people look similar or share resemblances. However, not everyone looks exactly the same. Children will inherit one set of gene instructions from their mother and another from their father. These combine, so that children will look a bit like each parent, but in their own unique way.

DID YOU KNOW?

Some genes, known as dominant, are stronger than others which are weaker, known as recessive. If both your parents have brown eyes, you will have brown eyes. If both your parents have blue eyes, you will have blue eyes. Simple, right? However, if one of your parents has brown eyes and the other blue eyes, you will have brown eyes. This is because the gene for brown eyes is dominant over the gene for blue eyes.

FACT

Sneezing in bright sunlight is an inherited trait.

Aaaaa-chooooo!

Lightbulb Moment!

Most mothers only have one baby at a time, but roughly one in every sixty births results in twins . . . just like Chris and Xand. There are two types of twins: identical and non-identical. Identical twins share exactly the same genes, whereas non-identical twins don't have exactly the same genes but are often still pretty similar in many ways.

FACT

The way you clasp your hands is inherited. 55% of people put their left thumb over their right thumb!

Having an identical twin also means you have a living, breathing reflection so that you can see yourself from every angle! Xand

FACT

One third of twins are identical (known as monozygotic twins), and two thirds are non-identical (known as dizygotic twins).

139

The Case of the MISSING MILK

Suspect 1: **Dad**

Suspect 2: **Chris**

Suspect 3: **Xand**

Chris, Xand and their dad were at home playing a game of charades.

Xand was thirsty and went to the fridge to get his favourite strawberry milkshake.

Oh no! Someone had finished Xand's strawberry milkshake!

Xand declared the area a crime scene and discovered saliva containing DNA on the bottle.

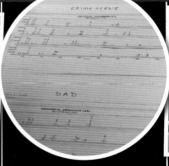

Xand took a swab from everyone to get their DNA so that he could find the culprit.

The DNA was tested at a special lab to find out whose DNA matched the saliva.

The results were in ... But who would it be? Dad? Chris? Xand?

It isn't Dad! His DNA did not match the swab taken from the bottle. However ...

Chris and Xand were both a match! That's because they are twins and share the same DNA.

Xand delivered the disappointing news that the case would remain unsolved.

Chris remembered that they had Fridge Cam CCTV in the kitchen, and ...

The footage revealed Xand sleepwalked to the fridge the previous night –

CASE CLOSED!

Look Closer

If you looked at your body under a microscope you would discover that it is made up of lots of very tiny, living building blocks that all join together to create you. These blocks are called cells. They come in all sorts of shapes and sizes.

SECRET CELLS

Organelles

Cytoplasm

Two for One

Mitosis is when cells divide and produce two identical cells. Cells do this for body growth and to replace old or damaged cells.

DID YOU KNOW?

Although cells vary in appearance, they pretty much all have the same basic structure, with an outer membrane, a jelly-like substance called cytoplasm which contains floating structures called organelles, and in the very centre a nucleus.

Nucleus

Cell Membrane

NAME: Red blood cells

STRUCTURE: Disc-shaped with central indentation, no nucleus

FUNCTION: Oxygen carrier

NAME: White blood cells

STRUCTURE: Often large, lobed

FUNCTION: Fight disease, clear up dead body cells

NAME: Muscle cells

STRUCTURE: Long

FUNCTION: Movement

NAME: Nerve cells, also known as neurons

STRUCTURE: Central nucleus with numerous projections

FUNCTION: Produce and carry electrical signals, known as impulses

NAME: Fat cells, also known as adipose cells

STRUCTURE: Big, bulky

FUNCTION: Energy stores, insulation, protection

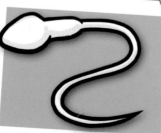

NAME: Sperm, also known as male sex cell or male gamete

STRUCTURE: Head, neck, middle piece and tail

FUNCTION: Reproduction

NAME: Egg, also known as ovum, female sex cell or female gamete

STRUCTURE: Large

FUNCTION: Reproduction

WHAT DID THE CELL SAY TO HIS SISTER WHEN SHE STEPPED ON HIS TOE?

I DON'T KNOW

MITOSIS!

Life Story

AGE: 0-1 month

NOTES: At the beginning, in your mother's womb, you were smaller than a grain of rice. At this stage you were known as an embryo made up from two layers of cells. It's from these cells that all your organs began to develop. By the end of the first month, you'd reached the size of a grain of rice.

AGE: 1-2 months

NOTES: From about eight weeks, you go from being called an embryo to a foetus and you're about the size of a kidney bean, moving constantly. You will have begun to form fingers, toes and eyes!

AGE: 2-3 months

NOTES: Rapidly growing, by now you were about 7-8cm long. Your fingernails and toenails would have started to appear at this age, along with tiny teeth.

AGE: 3-4 months

NOTES: At about 13cm long and weighing in at about 140g, you were able to suck your thumb, yawn and even pull faces! At this stage, doctors would have been able to tell whether you were a boy or a girl.

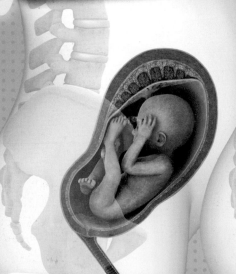

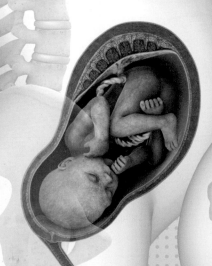

AGE: 4-5 months

NOTES: Constantly getting bigger, you now measured 27cm from head to toe. Not only that, but your hair would have been beginning to grow. Believe it or not, you would also have been starting to exercise – you wouldn't have been up to running a marathon, but you were stretching your muscles as they began to develop.

AGE: 5-6 months

NOTES: Weighing in at about 660g, you would have been beginning to put on fat, making your skin look less wrinkly as you filled out. And amazingly, your fingerprints would have now been visible too!

AGE: 6-7 months

NOTES: Now 40cm long, your senses would have been kicking into action, allowing you to hear things. Your hands started to become more active too and you were even able to cry.

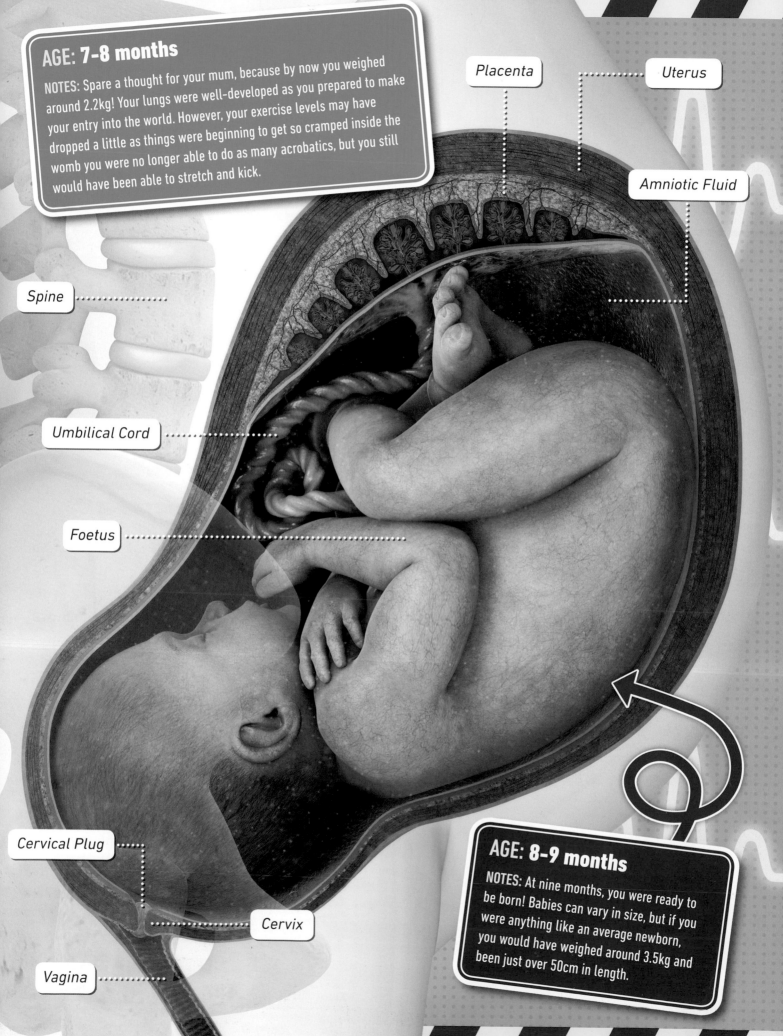

AGE: 7-8 months

NOTES: Spare a thought for your mum, because by now you weighed around 2.2kg! Your lungs were well-developed as you prepared to make your entry into the world. However, your exercise levels may have dropped a little as things were beginning to get so cramped inside the womb you were no longer able to do as many acrobatics, but you still would have been able to stretch and kick.

Placenta

Uterus

Amniotic Fluid

Spine

Umbilical Cord

Foetus

Cervical Plug

Cervix

Vagina

AGE: 8-9 months

NOTES: At nine months, you were ready to be born! Babies can vary in size, but if you were anything like an average newborn, you would have weighed around 3.5kg and been just over 50cm in length.

GROWING PAINS

Don't Worry

You've been growing since you were born, from a baby into a child. After you've been a child, the next stage is to become an adult. This phase where you turn from a child to an adult is called puberty and is something everyone goes through. It's completely normal and is nothing to be embarrassed about. You'll find that it happens to different people at slightly different ages, too. The main thing is not to worry.

He may look like an adult, but trust me, sometimes Xand still behaves like a child! Chris

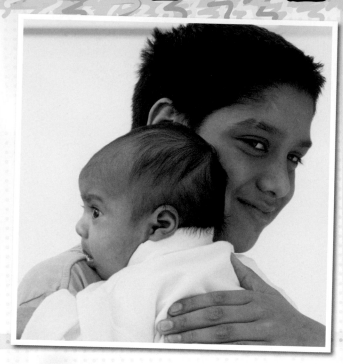

No Sweat!

It might seem a bit yucky, but everybody does it. Sweating is what your body does when you get too hot, and when that sweat evaporates, it takes heat away from your body and prevents your internal organs from overheating. During puberty, sweat glands become more active in your body. And when sweat comes into contact with the bacteria on your body, it can smell. So, on one hand sweat is pretty wonderful stuff because it helps to cool you down, but on the other hand it can be a bit whiffy!

FACT
Sweat glands are everywhere on your body except for your ears and lips.

Oh No, B.O.!

There are two types of sweat glands: eccrine and apocrine. The apocrine glands are in places like your groin and armpits. Bacteria love the sweat that is produced in these places because it contains high levels of protein and fatty acids. What you can smell isn't the sweat, but is actually bacteria poo! Don't worry, though – you can make sure you don't stay smelly by washing yourself (and your clothes) regularly.

FACT
The average person has about 2.5 million sweat glands.

FACT

During puberty, boys grow around 5–6cm per year.

Grow Up!

Hormones start telling your body to grow, making you taller and stronger. Other changes include boys getting broader and girls getting breasts.

Just be grateful you're not a baboon — they get giant red bottoms when they reach puberty! Chris

FACT

Some experts believe that puberty is brought on by a single gene called KiSS1.

FACT

The time between being a child and being an adult is called adolescence.

Rude Moods

When you're going through puberty, you can switch from being in a good mood to a bad mood extremely quickly. Or you might go from being very happy to really sad. And it's often for no particular reason. This is called a mood swing and it's completely normal. Once again, we have our hormones to blame as they change and adjust to adulthood.

Those pesky hormones have a lot to answer for if you ask me! Xand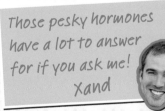

Things Just Got Hairy

You'll find hairs appearing where you didn't use to have them. Boys will start finding them on their faces, and everyone starts getting hair on their legs, armpits, and between their legs (we call this pubic hair). Some people keep all this extra hair, and some get rid of it. It's really up to you!

FACT

The coiled tube that stores sperm is called the epididymis and measures about 6m in length.

Hair Care

Hormone changes can stimulate your skin to produce more of an oil called sebum. This can make your hair more greasy. However, there are lots of things you can do to combat this, such as using special shampoos and styling products.

Balls!

This is a male-only part of puberty. Boys, your testicles will drop. They don't literally drop off – it's not that drastic! But they do lower within your scrotum as they grow a bit. It is an essential part of growing up, because your testicles start to make sperm, which are an essential part of making a baby when you're an adult. Sperm are cool. No, really. Your testicles hang lower outside your body to keep your sperm at the right temperature, which is slightly cooler than the rest of you. You might also find that one testicle hangs lower than the other (this is also perfectly normal and nothing to worry about!).

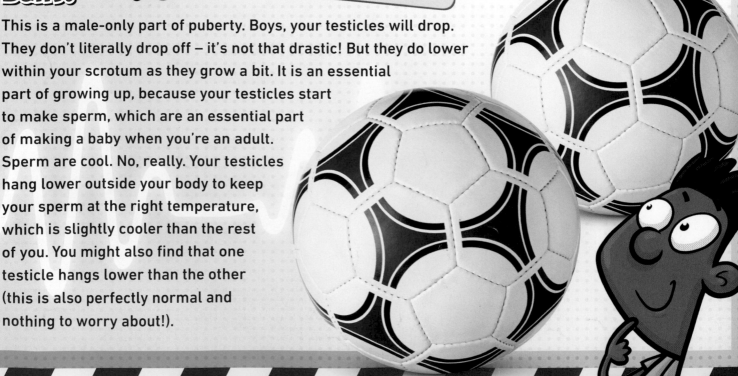

Spot On!

With the right amount of sebum you'll have nice, healthy, moist, glowing skin. Too much of the stuff and you can get a breakout of spots. During puberty, sebum levels can sky-rocket, which means some people will get a lot more spots than others. In severe cases, you might also get something called acne. However, help is at hand! Doctors can prescribe creams and tablets to fight severe acne. You can also help yourself by shampooing your hair regularly and avoid letting your hair fall across your face. You shouldn't wash any affected areas more than twice a day, and never, ever pick them!

Periods

Everyone gets a tummy ache from time to time, but there's a type of tummy ache that girls begin to get during puberty called their period. Don't panic. Your period will only last a few days at around the same time each month, and it's not always painful. Inside girls' bodies are two organs called ovaries, which produce eggs. Eggs are among the things needed to make a baby when you're an adult. Babies grow in a place called a womb. Wombs have a lining that gets made each month, known as your menstrual cycle. However, when there's no baby, the lining isn't needed and comes out as a bit of blood. When it first starts, tell an adult who you trust and they'll be able to give you help and advice.

FACT
Girls are born with about two million eggs, around 300,000 of which survive to puberty.

WHY DID THE TEENAGER PUT HIS SKIN IN PRISON?

I DON'T KNOW

HE DIDN'T WANT A BREAKOUT!

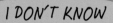

INSIDE'S OUTSIDE

Wow!

Before 1895, the only way that doctors could have had a look inside you would have been to cut you open! Thankfully, a German physicist called Wilhelm Röntgen realized how useful X-radiation was for seeing what was going on inside our bodies. He also came up with the term 'X-ray'.

So X-ray isn't short for Xand ray? That's disappointing! Xand

FACT
The 'X' in X-ray means 'unknown'.

Amazing!

Magnetic Resonance Imaging is usually known by a much snappier name: MRI. It's a brilliant piece of technology used to see inside places like your brain. An MRI machine is a bit like a bed in a magnetic tunnel. The magnet applies a pulsed field to make the protons in your body line up in the same direction, a bit like the way a magnet can make the needle in a compass face in its direction. The radio signals that are released are analysed by a computer, and an image is made.

Cool CATs

CT scans are also known as CAT scans. The name comes from the Computerized Tomography scanner which is used to build up 3D images of the body. The scanner rotates around your body, sending out X-rays. Each image is like a separate slice in a loaf of bread. The computer puts the slices together and a 3D image of your body is produced.

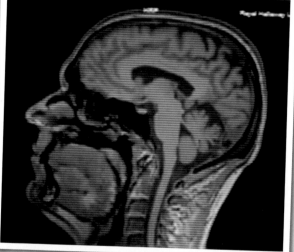

Echo ... Echo ... Echo ...

When doctors need a scan, but don't want to send radiation through the body, they can use something called an ultrasound. When your mum was pregnant with you, an ultrasound might even have been the first way she saw you! Ultrasound creates 3D images by beaming high-pitched sound waves into the body. They bounce off tissue and create echoes that a clever computer can turn into an image.

BABY'S FACE

XAND WAS CARRYING THE RESULTS OF VARIOUS CT SCANS, X-RAYS AND MRI SCANS WHEN HE TRIPPED AND MUDDLED THEM UP.

Hi-Tech Hiccup

CAN YOU MATCH THE IMAGE OF THE BODY TO THE RIGHT PART OF THE PATIENT?

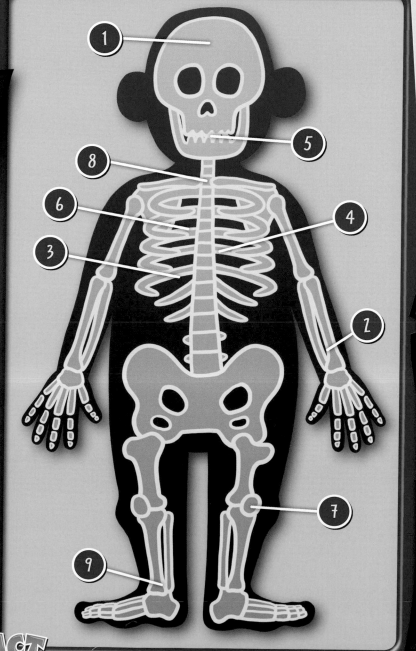

FACT
Ultrasound is the name given to sound waves that have frequencies greater than 20,000Hz. It's too high-pitched for human hearing, but many animals (including dogs, cats and bats) can hear ultrasound.

FACT
X-rays can be used to study things like Egyptian mummies without damaging them.

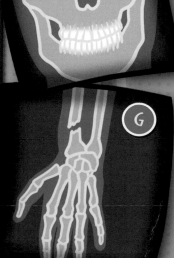

TURN TO PAGE 173 TO FIND OUT IF YOU WERE RIGHT!

DiY SPARE PARTS

DO YOU WANT TO CREATE A PERFECT REPLICA OF YOUR SKULL?
NO PROBLEM! FOLLOW THIS SIMPLE STEP-BY-STEP GUIDE TO 3D PRINTING!*

STEP 1

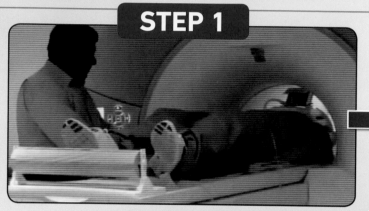

Have an MRI scan done of your head.

STEP 2

Save the image to a memory stick.

STEP 3

Put memory stick into a computer attached to a 3D printer. They are capable of printing all kinds of body parts.

STEP 5

YOUR SKULL IS COMPLETE!

STEP 4

Wait while the printer creates your skull, layer by layer.

When I had my skull made I discovered that I actually have a very small hole in the back of my skull — wow! Chris

*Terms and conditions apply. You will need to buy or borrow a 3D printer. Might be cheaper and easier not to create a perfect replica of your skull and just carry on reading instead.

150

TACKLING TUMOURS

Lightbulb Moment!

Bodies are made up of billions of cells, but sometimes they can go wrong. And that's what a tumour is: a bunch of cells that are no longer growing properly. Doctors use beams of energy called radiation to destroy bad tumours. Unfortunately, sometimes nice normal cells living close by can get destroyed by the radiation too.

Beams of energy blasted at baddies to destroy them? Pass the popcorn, this sounds like a sci-fi film! Xand

Meet Gary!

Gary is a special robot that is able to deliver a beam of radiation as thin as a pin that's so precise it avoids the good cells and targets only the bad ones.

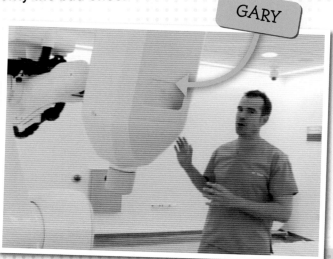

GARY

Hedgehogs!

Some doctors call this image a hedgehog, and you can see why! You'll probably be able to make out the spinal column and hips. What you can also see is a tumour, shown in pink. The blue lines each represent one dose of radiation being beamed in from Gary to attack the tumour. The hedgehog is essentially a map showing doctors where each beam of radiation will be going in.

Robo Surgery

Patients lie down for about 45 minutes whilst Gary gets to work. Gary moves to each position, delivers a dose of radiation, as mapped out by the hedgehog, and then repositions to the next place.

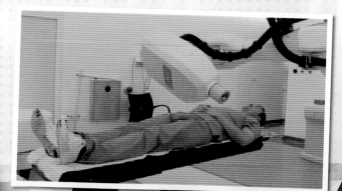

Beam Me Up!

Using his laser eye to guide him, Gary is able to attack the tumour cells from many different angles and avoid the good, healthy cells.

GIGANTIC GERMS

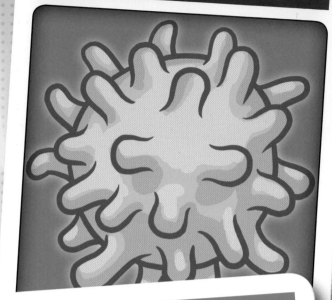

Microscopic Menaces

When you think of what a cold looks like, you might picture someone sneezing or with a runny nose. But have you wondered what the actual cold virus looks like? Let's put some common viruses and germs under the microscope!

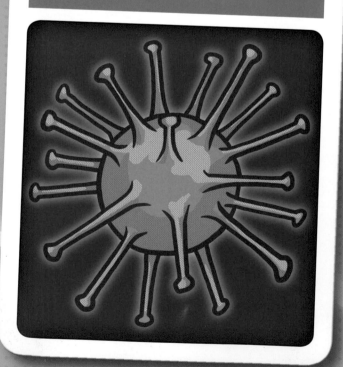

I don't know about you, Ouch! fans, but I reckon some of them look like aliens from outer space! Xand

CHICKEN POX VIRUS

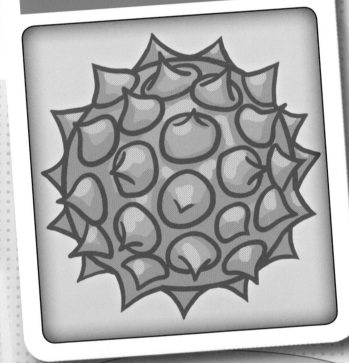

FLU VIRUS

WHAT'S THE DIFFERENCE BETWEEN BIRD FLU AND SWINE FLU?

I DON'T KNOW

IF YOU HAVE BIRD FLU YOU NEED TWEETMENT AND IF YOU HAVE SWINE FLU YOU NEED OINKMENT!

152

MEASLES VIRUS

MUMPS VIRUS

RUBELLA VIRUS

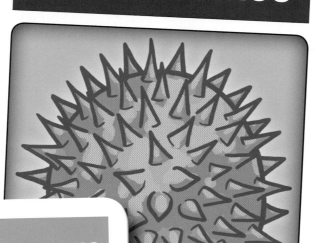

FACT

Once a virus is inside a cell it can make hundreds of thousands of copies of itself.

GLANDULAR FEVER VIRUS

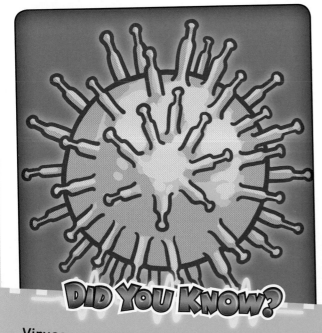

CONJUNCTIVITIS VIRUS

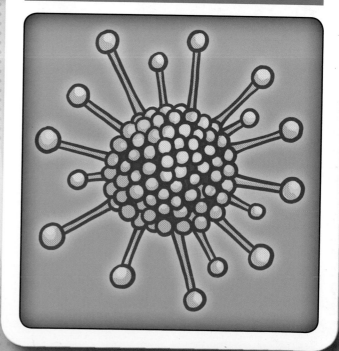

DID YOU KNOW?

Viruses are even smaller than bacteria and require living hosts – such as people, plants or animals – to multiply. Otherwise, they can't survive. When a virus enters your body, it invades some of your cells and takes over the cell machinery, redirecting it to produce the virus.

A Day in the Life of Dr Chris

NICE SUIT!

Although this suit might make Chris look like he's getting ready to be blasted into outer space, it's actually called PPE, or personal protective equipment. It's used so that doctors and nurses can treat patients with serious infections, without getting ill themselves. You might have seen suits like this on the news during outbreaks of viruses like Ebola in West Africa. These things make the news because they are serious, but they're also very rare.

BODY BURGLAR

An infectious disease like a virus is similar to a burglar who's found exactly the right spanner to break into the security system that usually protects your cells. Once the virus has broken in, it is able to infect the cells. Scientists like Chris want to find out which spanner the virus uses to unlock the cell. Then they can stop the spanner working and create medicine to make people better.

MUTANT MAKERS

To understand how viruses work, scientists make mutants. This is done by taking the original virus and changing one thing about it, a bit like slightly altering the shape of the spanner the virus is using to break into your cells' security system.

CLEVER STUFF

The mutant samples are added to healthy human cells to see which one is able to infect them. Take a look at these uninfected cells that are nice and healthy, with no virus on them. There are lots and lots of them.

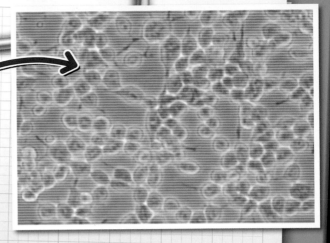

These cells have been infected with the original virus. You can see that they are clumped together, floating around, and there are far fewer of them. Under a special green light, you can see all the infected cells. This proves that this virus has the right spanner to infect the cells!

Here are the cells that have been infected with the first mutant version of the virus. They are floating around and look pretty similar to the original virus. This mutant obviously still has the right spanner to infiltrate the cells!

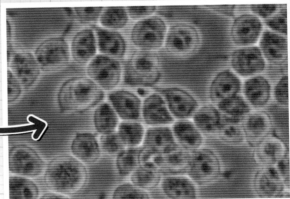

In the second mutant we have really healthy cells, and lots of them too! And under the green light, the virus doesn't show up at all. The virus has been changed so that it no longer has a spanner that can break into the cells and infect them.

LIFE SAVERS

It can take a long time to find the right mutation and there are lots of diseases that scientists still don't understand and haven't found the right 'spanners' for. However, research has led to some major breakthroughs that have saved a lot of lives across the world.

For Your Appointment

How Do You Feel?

From time to time, almost everyone feels unwell and you may need to visit your local doctor's surgery. Some people find this a scary place, but actually they are there to make you feel better so you shouldn't worry about going to see the doctor.

Most of us doctors are actually pretty nice people and we're really not that scary! Xand

Who's Who?

When you visit your doctor, the building is usually called a surgery, GP practice or health centre. Lots of people work there who all have different jobs including GP (general practitioner), nurse, healthcare assistant, receptionist and practice manager.

Great Person

GP might officially stand for general practitioner, but it could also stand for 'great person'! They treat all kinds of common medical conditions, from colds to verrucas, diabetes to ear infections. If they think that you need a medicine to make you better, they will write a special letter called a prescription that you can take to a pharmacy to get the medication. They can also suggest you go to hospital if you need more urgent or specialist care.

Nice Nurses

In a GP practice, nurses play an important part in providing care for patients. You might even see a nurse instead of a GP for some things. Nurses are able to give you an injection if you need one and can also do things like check your height and weight.

Tip Top Teeth

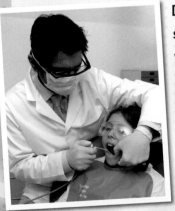

Dentists are usually based in their own surgeries and are like special doctors who just look after your dental (teeth) and oral (mouth) care. They will look out for any disease that you may have and can provide treatments such as fillings. They'll also advise on whether you need to have braces if your teeth aren't coming through completely straight.

DOCTOR, DOCTOR, I FEEL LIKE A BRIDGE

WHAT'S COME OVER YOU?

THREE CARS, A LORRY AND TWO BUSES!

Bag of Tricks

Amazing!

It's time to have a look at some of the instruments and tools that a doctor might pick from their bag of tricks to find out how to make you feel well again.

Stethoscopes

Stethoscopes let doctors listen to your heartbeat and also to your lungs. If they hear something out of the ordinary, they may want to do more investigating.

Thermometer

Doctors and nurses use a thermometer to find out your temperature. It should be around 37°C. If it is higher, it might mean that you have a fever and your body is fighting an infection.

Tongue Depressor

A tongue depressor is a flat wooden stick – a bit like one you'd have left after eating an ice lolly. A doctor uses it to make your tongue flat so that they can have a better look inside your mouth and throat.

Otoscope

An otoscope or auriscope lets doctors look inside your ears, nose and throat. It's even got a little light so that they can see better and spot any signs of infection.

Sphygmomanometer

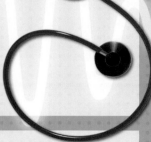

This is a really long word for a blood pressure meter! Doctors use it to see how hard your heart is pumping blood through your body. The cuff is placed on your arm and gets tighter and tighter to measure this. Blood pressure can be too high or too low.

Ophthalmoscope

Doctors use an ophthalmoscope (pronounced 'off-thalmoscope') to shine a light in your eye, and make sure that everything is healthy.

And finally ...

One of a doctor's most important tools is their hands! For example, if you have a pain in your tummy, your doctor may want to have a feel because there is lots of important stuff in that area and they need to make sure they can't feel anything out of the ordinary. Doctors can also use their hands to 'palpate and percuss' (which means tapping on you to see if you sound hollow and not hollow in the right places!).

EMERGENCY!

Busy, Busy, Busy

If you're lucky, you may never be one of over 20 million people who visit the emergency department in UK hospitals each year. They are open 24 hours a day, 7 days a week, 365 days a year, and deal with genuine medical emergencies.

Emergency Department A & E

999

It is normally only adults who have to call 999 in an emergency. However, there may be times when you have to make the call for others. You should only call 999 in a genuine emergency. The person who answers your call will ask you some questions so they can understand the situation and what help you need.

What Happens?

When you get to the emergency department, you will have to let the people at reception know what is wrong with you. Some hospitals even have a separate children's emergency department. Once you have registered, a nurse or doctor will see you to assess how serious your condition is. This is called triage and makes sure that the most serious problems are seen fastest. Next you will either receive treatment at the hospital, be moved to somewhere better suited to your condition, or sent home if you don't need further care.

EMERGENCY CALL
999

The ambulance service uses lots of different vehicles, not just ambulances. They also have rapid response vehicles including cars, motorcycles and bikes. Depending on where you are and how far away from a hospital the emergency is, an air ambulance, which is a helicopter, might also be sent.

Emergency Ambulance

7690

London Ambulance Service
NHS Trust

NHS

PARAMEDIC

On Call

Chris and Xand have spent time on call with Jan Vann who's a paramedic with the West Midlands Ambulance Service. Jan's rapid response vehicle is one of over 800 vehicles serving 5 million people. Paramedics like Jan are often one of the first at the scene of an emergency. This fast medical service is on standby ready to help you 24 hours a day. The ambulance service takes thousands of 999 calls. Jan alone can attend 20 emergency callouts in a day!

And a lovely person Jan Vann is too — we're thinking of starting her fan club! Chris & Xand

FIRST AID →

What is First Aid?

At some stage, most people have an accident and hurt themselves. When someone is injured or becomes unwell suddenly, they need someone who knows what to do. First aid is all about helping people in situations like this. The next few pages will tell you about some of the first aid that you can use to help people, but if you are ever worried, it's best to get an adult or call 999.

WHAT SHOULD YOU DO IF YOU KNOCK OUT ONE OF YOUR ADULT TEETH?

A Get a pointed black hat and enter a fancy-dress competition as a witch?

B Ring the tooth fairy helpline?

C Stop the bleeding and put the tooth in a glass of milk?

The answer is C. If you've lost a tooth, stop the bleeding by applying pressure to the hole with something like a clean cloth. You should put the tooth in a glass of milk because it helps keep the tooth alive longer before you visit the dentist who might be able to put the tooth back in.

WHAT SHOULD YOU DO IF YOU GET A BURN?

A Hop up and down and tap it with a wand?

B Ask it politely to stop hurting?

C Run it under cold water?

The answer is C. Run it under the cold tap as quickly as possible and keep it there for a good ten minutes to cool the burn down.

WHAT SHOULD YOU DO IF YOU FALL OFF YOUR BIKE IN THE PARK AND BREAK YOUR ARM?

A Run around the park, screaming 'Aaah! My arm's broken!'?

B Support it to stop it moving using your hand and clothing or cushions?

C Tell your teacher that you won't ever be able to do homework again?

*The answer is B. If you think that you might have broken your arm, support it to stop it moving using your hand, clothing or cushions, **and tell an adult or call 999.***

WHAT SHOULD YOU DO TO TREAT A BUMP ON THE HEAD?

A Try and press the bump back in again?

B Eat four bags of crisps to cheer yourself up?

C Put something cold on the bump?

The answer is C. You should put something cold on it like a bag of frozen peas for no longer than ten minutes. Make sure that there is something like a clean tea towel between your skin and the bag of frozen peas. The frozen peas will reduce the pain and swelling, but if you feel sick or dizzy you should tell an adult.

WHAT SHOULD YOU DO IF YOU THINK THAT SOMEONE IS UNCONSCIOUS, BUT STILL BREATHING?

A Tip their head back, check they are breathing and roll them on to their side?

B Shout 'Wakey! Wakey!' really loudly?

C Lie down next to them and have a sleep, enjoying the peace and quiet?

The answer is A. If someone has been knocked unconscious and they're breathing, tip their head back to check they are breathing, gently roll them on to one side and find an adult.

. . . AND DON'T FORGET, ALL THESE FIRST AID TIPS ARE WHAT TO DO IN AN EMERGENCY. IT'S ALWAYS BEST TO FIND AN ADULT IF YOU CAN OR CALL 999.

FIRST AID →

WHAT SHOULD YOU DO IF YOU GET A SPLINTER IN YOUR HAND?

A Train some ants to crawl over your hand and drag the splinter out?

B Clean it with water and ask an adult to remove it?

C Ignore it, and never use that hand again for the rest of your life?

The answer is B. Wash the area and get an adult to remove the splinter with a pair of tweezers. Then you should wash the area again and put a plaster on it.

WHAT SHOULD YOU DO IF YOU SEE SOMEONE CHOKING?

A Act quickly by hitting them on the back up to five times?

B Ask them politely to speak more clearly?

C Send a small and expertly trained mouse into their mouth and get it to push the blockage from the other side?

The answer is A. Hit them on the back between their shoulder blades up to five times. Choking can be very serious, so it's always best to find an adult.

WHAT SHOULD YOU DO IF YOU GET STUNG BY A BEE?

A Run around, screaming 'I want my teddy!'?

B Go and have some cake?

C Scrape off the sting and put something cold on the area for no more than ten minutes?

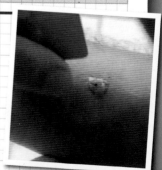

The answer is C. First of all, scrape out the sting with something like a credit card or your nail – the sting will probably be sticking out and will look like a splinter. Then, put something cold on the area, like a bag of frozen peas, but remember to put something like a clean tea towel between your skin and the bag of frozen peas. You should only do this for a maximum of ten minutes.

WHAT SHOULD YOU DO IF YOU ACCIDENTALLY GET SOMETHING NASTY IN YOUR EYE?

A Wrap your whole head in bandages and pretend you're an Egyptian mummy?

B Order another eye online from Eyes R Us?

C Wash your eye out with lukewarm water?

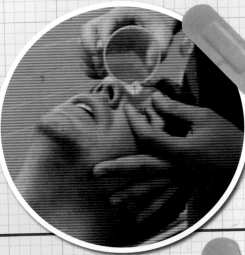

The answer is C. Sit the patient down, gently hold open the eye and pour water right on to the eyeball – and always try to find an adult.

HOW SHOULD YOU TREAT A CARPET BURN ON YOUR KNEE?

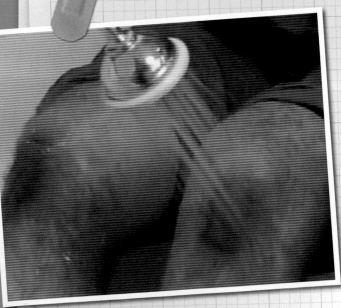

A Blow on your knee for at least five years?

B Put it under cold running water for at least ten minutes?

C Rip up all the carpets because they are clearly very dangerous?

The answer is B. If you get a carpet burn, run it under cold water for at least ten minutes.

. . . AND DON'T FORGET, ALL THESE FIRST AID TIPS ARE WHAT TO DO IN AN EMERGENCY. IT'S ALWAYS BEST TO FIND AN ADULT IF YOU CAN OR CALL 999.

FIRST AID →

WHAT SHOULD YOU DO IF SOMEONE IS REALLY COLD AND YOU THINK THAT THEY MIGHT HAVE HYPOTHERMIA?

A Use them as a giant ice cube in your drink?

B Warm the person by wrapping them in a blanket, and give them warm drinks and chocolate?

C Enter them into a talent show as a novelty shivering act?

The answer is B. If you think someone has hypothermia, you should warm the person by wrapping a blanket or towel around them, and give them warm drinks and high-energy food such as chocolate.

WHAT SHOULD YOU DO IF YOU GET A NOSEBLEED?

A Make patterns with the dripping blood?

B Lean forward and pinch the soft part of your nose for ten minutes?

C Grab some garlic in case there are any vampires around?

The answer is B. If you have a bleeding nose, the best thing to do is sit quietly, lean forward and pinch the soft bit of your nose for ten minutes while you breathe through your mouth. And remember, it probably looks a lot worse than it actually is.

WHAT SHOULD YOU DO IF YOU TRAP AND BADLY CUT YOUR FINGER?

A Use a clean cloth to apply pressure and stop the bleeding?

B Send in an army of ants to stitch it back up?

C Show your teacher and see if they freak out?

The answer is A. Use a clean cloth to apply pressure and stop the bleeding. If the fingertip has come off, you should put it in a clean bag, then put the bag on ice and tell an adult. You should then go to hospital or call 999.

WHAT SHOULD YOU DO TO TREAT A BRUISED FOOT?

A Build a time machine, go back to before the accident happened and try to prevent it?

B Remove the bruised foot?

C Simply apply something cold for no longer than ten minutes to relieve the pain?

WHAT SHOULD YOU DO IF YOU BREAK YOUR LEG?

A Ask your mum if she'll carry you around the house for six months?

B Support the injured leg to keep it still and call 999?

C Chop the leg off – it's no use now it's broken?

The answer is C. Put something cold on it, like a bag of frozen peas, to relieve the pain and reduce the swelling. And remember, always put something like a clean tea towel between your skin and the frozen peas, and never do this for longer than ten minutes.

The answer is B. If you think you might have broken your leg, support it to stop it moving using anything that's handy and tell an adult or call 999.

. . . AND DON'T FORGET, ALL THESE FIRST AID TIPS ARE WHAT TO DO IN AN EMERGENCY. IT'S ALWAYS BEST TO FIND AN ADULT IF YOU CAN OR CALL 999.

FIRST AID →

WHAT SHOULD YOU DO IF YOU ACCIDENTALLY GET WHACKED IN THE EYE?

A Shut your other eye and hope everything's OK when you open them both?

B Make an eye-patch and pretend you're a pirate?

C Put something cold on your eye for no more than ten minutes to relieve the pain?

The answer is C. Put something cold on it, like a bag of frozen peas, to relieve the pain and reduce the swelling. And remember, always put something like a clean tea towel between your skin and the frozen peas, and never do this for longer than ten minutes. If you've got problems with your vision, you should ask an adult to take you to Accident & Emergency as soon as possible.

WHAT SHOULD YOU DO IF YOU HAVE A BLEEDING GASH ON YOUR HEAD?

A Wrap 100m of toilet roll round your head?

B Immediately do a zombie impression?

C Apply pressure immediately to stop the bleeding and tell an adult?

The answer is C. If you have a bleeding gash on your head, use a piece of cloth or your clothing to apply pressure to stop the bleeding. Sit the patient down if they're feeling faint and tell an adult.

WHAT SHOULD YOU DO IF YOU TRAP YOUR FINGER IN A DOOR?

A Hit a bone on all your other fingers to match them all up?

B Tell your teacher you can't do any writing again, ever?

C Apply something cold to the finger?

The answer is C. Put something cold on it, like a bag of frozen peas, to relieve the pain and reduce the swelling. And remember, always put something like a clean tea towel between your skin and the frozen peas, and never do this for longer than ten minutes.

WHAT SHOULD YOU DO IF YOU SPRAIN YOUR ANKLE WHILST IN THE PARK?

A Roll around on the grass, crying?

B Apply something cold to the injury for no longer than ten minutes?

C Buy the Ankle De-Sprainer 2000 and hope it works?

The correct answer is B. You need to reduce the pain and the swelling with a cold compress. But remember, you shouldn't do this for any longer than ten minutes!

WHAT SHOULD YOU DO WITH A SUSPECTED BROKEN FINGER?

A Take a selfie of it and send it to your friends?

B Elevate the finger and support it?

C Stick it in a glass of lemonade and let the bubbles soothe it?

The answer is B. When you break bones they bleed and you get swelling under the skin and that's partly what hurts. If you put the hand up, less blood can get to it and all you have to do is put your hand above your heart because your heart's where all the blood comes from.

... AND DON'T FORGET, ALL THESE FIRST AID TIPS ARE WHAT TO DO IN AN EMERGENCY. IT'S ALWAYS BEST TO FIND AN ADULT IF YOU CAN OR CALL 999.

Spare Parts

Have you ever had a toy or game that you've had to build or put together yourself? And then when you're done, there are still some spare parts that don't appear to do anything? Well, your body has bits just like this too!

A Not So Tall Tail

Found at the very end of your spine is your coccyx. It also has another name, your tailbone, which might explain a bit more about what it is. Many believe your coccyx is what remains of our distant ancestors' tails! When our ancestors learnt how to walk upright, there was no longer a need for a tail so it gradually got smaller and all that's left now is our useless coccyx.

Useless App

If you've ever used a smart phone, you're bound to have come across a useless app that doesn't ever get used. Well, your body has a useless app too. A useless app-endix, to be precise. The appendix is between the small intestine and large intestine, but it has nothing to do with digestion. If you're lucky, you may never even have to think about yours, but in some people it can become inflamed and infected. In extreme cases, it can rupture or burst when someone develops appendicitis.

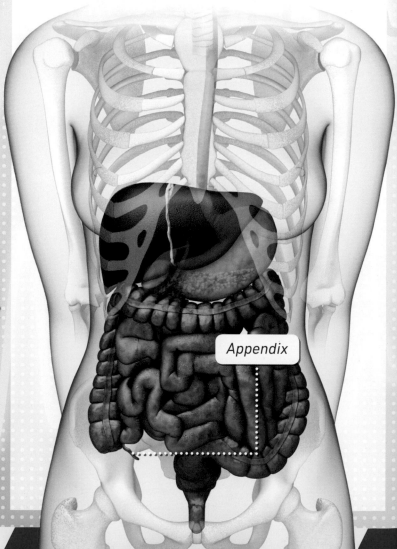

Appendix

If I'm honest, I'm a bit disappointed that we don't still have tails – I reckon I'd look really good with one! Xand

Nothing Wise About These Teeth

Wisdom teeth are located at the very back of your mouth. They usually develop between the ages of 17 and 25 years old. They often come through at odd angles and can be quite painful. In fact, only 5% of people develop trouble-free wisdom teeth, and 35% don't grow them at all. Not good news for the other 60%!

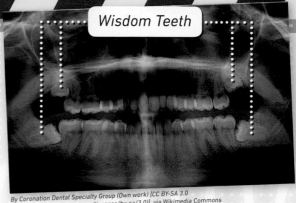

Wisdom Teeth

By Coronation Dental Specialty Group (Own work) [CC BY-SA 3.0 (http://creativecommons.org/licenses/by-sa/3.0)], via Wikimedia Commons

No Point!

One in ten people have a small, pointed fold of skin on their upper ear called a Darwin's point or Darwin's tubercle. Scientists aren't sure why some people have this, but some think it might have been a joint that allowed the ear to swivel or flop down.

DARWIN'S POINT

Wiggly Ears

Auricular muscles surround the outer ear. Some animals use them to move their ears towards the direction of sound. Humans have these muscles, but unless you have the ability to wiggle your ears, your auricular muscles serve no purpose.

The Trouble with Tonsils

Although it might be true that tonsils can help fight germs, most people only become aware of their tonsils when they become infected. As we found out on page 34, lots of people, including Xand, have them removed and don't miss them at all!

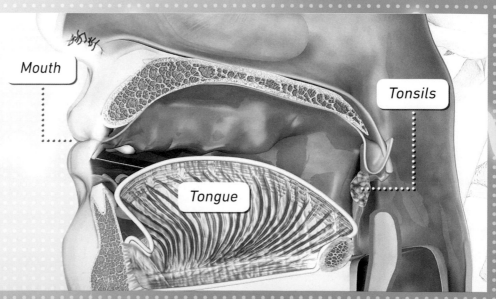

Mouth

Tonsils

Tongue

The A-Z of You

OPERATION → Ouch!

Hello again, *Ouch!* fans,

You've almost reached the end of the *Operation Ouch! HuManual*. Hopefully now you've got a better idea of how your body works and, more importantly, how to get the most out of it.

We thought it would be a good idea to end with a glossary of some of our favourite medical terms. They'll help you on your way to becoming an *Ouch!* expert – and they're also here because we think they're cool!

Which one's your favourite?

Chris
Xand

Dr Chris & Dr Xand

GLOSSARY →

Abscess – a collection of pus

Allergy – a reaction caused by your immune system to something (especially food, pollen, fur or dust) to which your body has become very sensitive

Antibiotic – medicine that attacks bacteria that make you unwell

Bacteria – a group of micro-organisms, some of which cause disease

Borborygmus – a rumbling tummy, usually signifying you are hungry

Bruxism – grinding your teeth

Cartilage – a connective tissue that covers the ends of bones in joints

Cell – one of over 35 trillion microscopic living units that make up your body

Chromosome – one of 46 thread-like structures in a cell's nucleus

Cilia – microscopic, hair-like projections from certain body cells

Contagious – when an illness is contagious, it means one person can catch it from another

Dehydration – when there isn't enough water in your body

Diagnosis – the term used for when doctors find out what medical issue you have

Eczema – a condition that can make your skin red, itchy and dry

Fasciculation – when your muscles twitch in places like your eyelids

Fever – when your body gets hotter than normal on the inside

Flu – short for influenza, a virus that can make you feel tired, achy and generally not very well

Frenulum – the piece of skin that attaches your tongue to the bottom of your mouth

Gastric juices – these begin to break down food in your stomach as part of the digestive process

Gene – one of 20,000 instructions contained within the DNA of a cell's nucleus

Gingivitis – gum disease

Gland – a group of cells that produce a substance that is released into or on to your body

Gustatory rhinitis – a runny nose caused by spicy food

Hormone – a chemical messenger

Horripilation – goosebumps

Immune system – a collection of cells that protect the body from diseases

Injection – when a doctor uses a needle to put a medicine or vaccine into your body

Keratin – a hard protein found in hair, nails and skin

Laparoscopy – a kind of surgery that uses a tiny camera to look inside your body

Ligaments – bands of connective tissue that hold bones together at joints

Macrophage – a type of white blood cell that engulfs and destroys pathogens that cause disease

Mitosis – a type of cell division that produces two identical cells, used in growth and replacement of damaged or worn-out cells

Morsicatio buccarum – when you bite the inside of your cheek

Mucus – a thick, slimy substance that protects and lubricates different parts of the body

Muscle – a type of body tissue that contracts, or gets shorter, to produce movement

Nocturnal enuresis – this is what it's called if you wet the bed at night

Nucleus – the centre of a cell that contains DNA

Organ – a part of the body made up of two or more types of tissue that has a specific role or roles

Orthostatic hypotension – the dizzy head rush you might get if you stand up too quickly

Pathogen – a type of micro-organism, including bacteria and viruses, that causes disease

Rhinovirus – the virus that causes the common cold

Sphenopalatine ganglioneuralgia – brain freeze when you eat ice-cream too fast

Sternutate – to sneeze

Synchronous diaphragmatic flutter – a hiccup

Tinnitus – ringing in your ears caused by loud noise or an infection

Tissue – a group of one type, or similar types, of cells that work together to perform a particular function

Transient diaphragmatic spasm – this is the fancy term for being hit and winded, it feels scary but doesn't last for long

Vasovagal syncope – fainting caused by things like seeing blood or hearing shocking news

Virus – a type of germ that can make you unwell

Zoonosis – any disease that humans can get from animals

Answers

Page 19 – THE EYE TEST

Page 27 – WORD SEARCH

Page 43 – THE SMELLING TEST

1. C. nasal cartilage
2. B. 100mph
3. A. sinuses
4. A. your mouth
5. C. salty
6. B. about 10,000
7. B. about 7cm
8. C. about 40 million
9. B. a cup
10. B. soot

Page 49 – CHILLED TO THE BONE

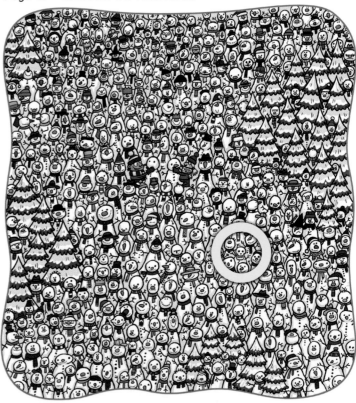

Page 59 – MUSCLE OR MUSSEL?

MUSCLES: Gluteus maximus, Pectoralis major, Deltoid, Gastrocnemius, Rectus abdominus

MUSSELS: Mytilus galloprovincialis, Modiolus modiolus, Perna canaliculus, Mytilus chilensis, Mytilus edulis

Page 67 – SPOT TO SPOT

It's Xand, of course!

Page 89 – THE BLOOD TEST

1. A. the left side and right side
2. B. a fist
3. A. veins
4. A. 5 litres
5. C. 125
6. B. 2.5 billion
7. C. a stethoscope
8. B. 2.5 times
9. False
10. A. one minute

Page 95 – CITY OR SEASIDE?

Sample *1* is from the seaside and *2* is from the city.

Page 97 – LUNG FUN

1. C. windpipe
2. B. 20,000
3. A. snot
4. C. 300 million
5. True
6. B. dogs
7. C. trachea
8. A. spirometer
9. C. about 8,000–9,000
10. B. can float on water

Page 109 – PICK A POO

HEALTHY POO: HIGH-FIBRE WHOLEMEAL BREAD, BOTTLED WATER, SWEETCORN, BAKED BEANS, BROCCOLI, APPLES, WHOLEMEAL PASTA, BANANAS

DIARRHOEA: NASTY BACTERIA

CONSTIPATION: WHITE BREAD, DEEP-FRIED CHICKEN, CAKE, ICE-CREAM, FROZEN CHIPS

Page 117 – AMAZING MAZE

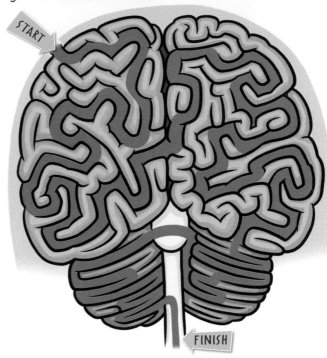

Page 137 – SNAKES AND (DNA) LADDERS

Page 149 – HI-TECH HICCUP

1 = D
2 = G
3 = A
4 = H
5 = C
6 = B
7 = E
8 = F
9 = I